PICTURE BOOK OF
BIRDS

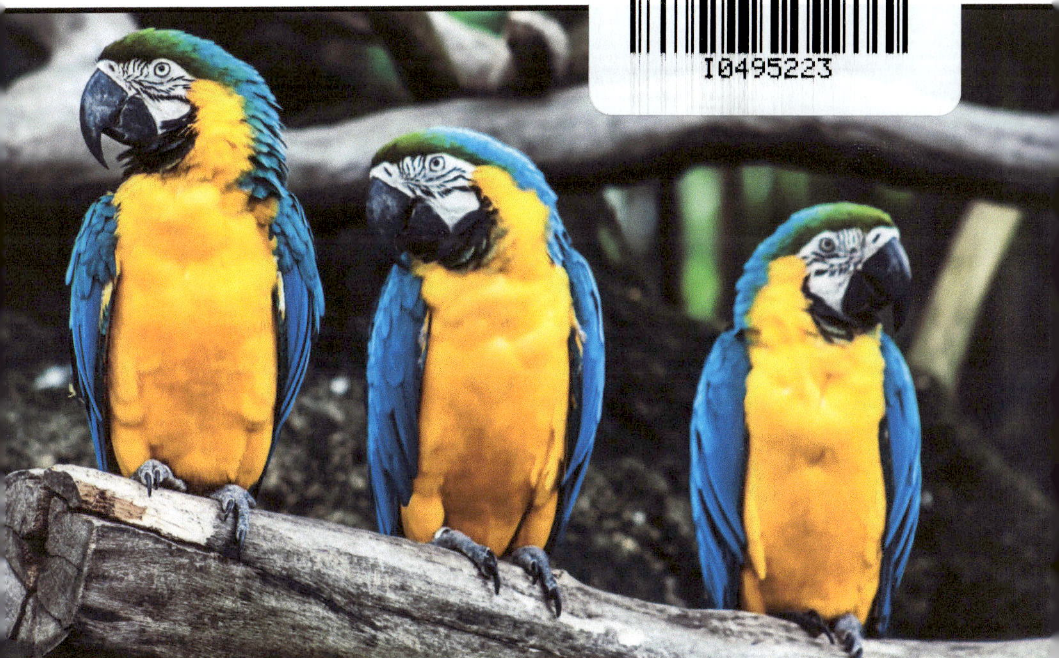

MIGHTY OAK BOOKS

Copyright © 2019 Mighty Oak Books
All Rights Reserved.

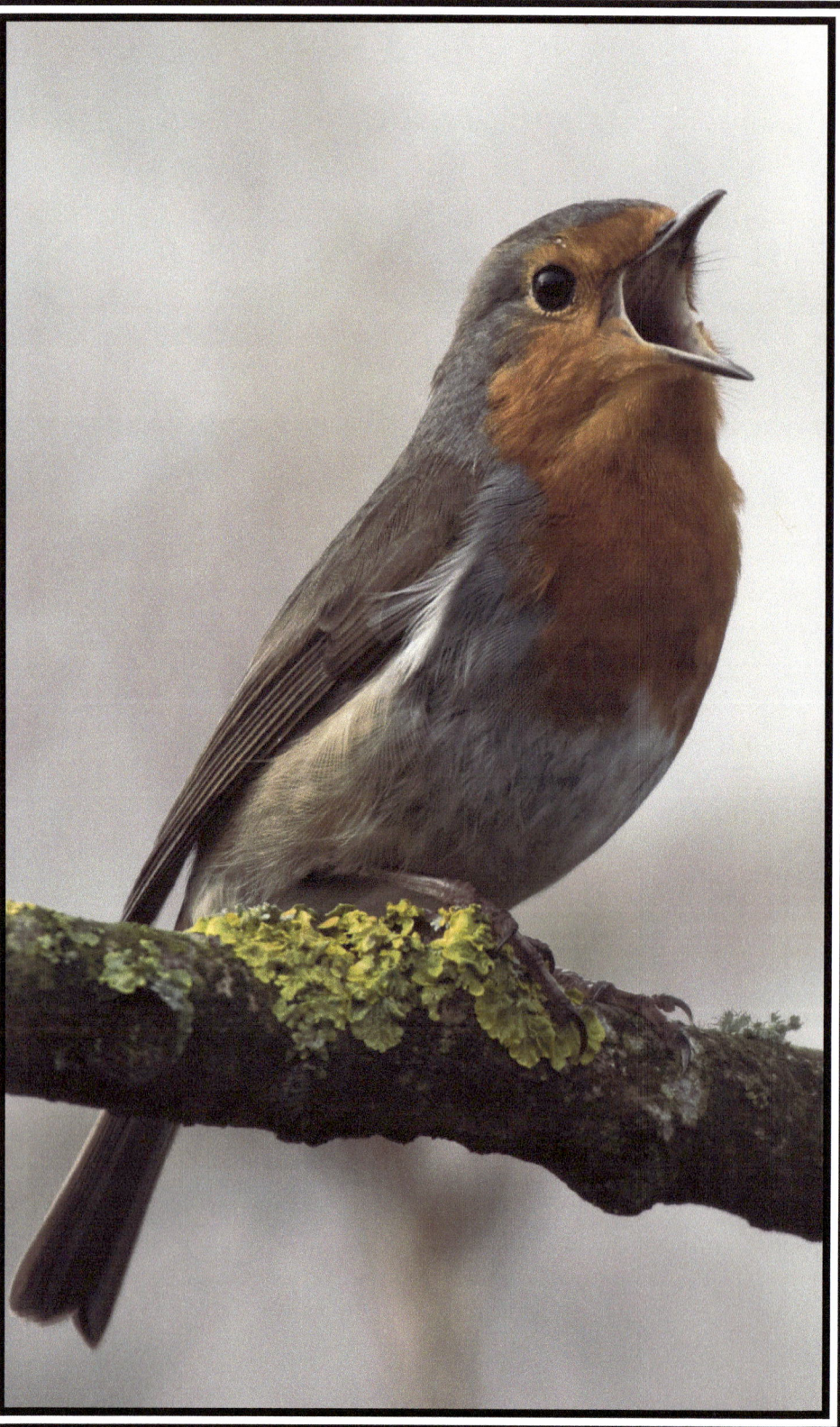

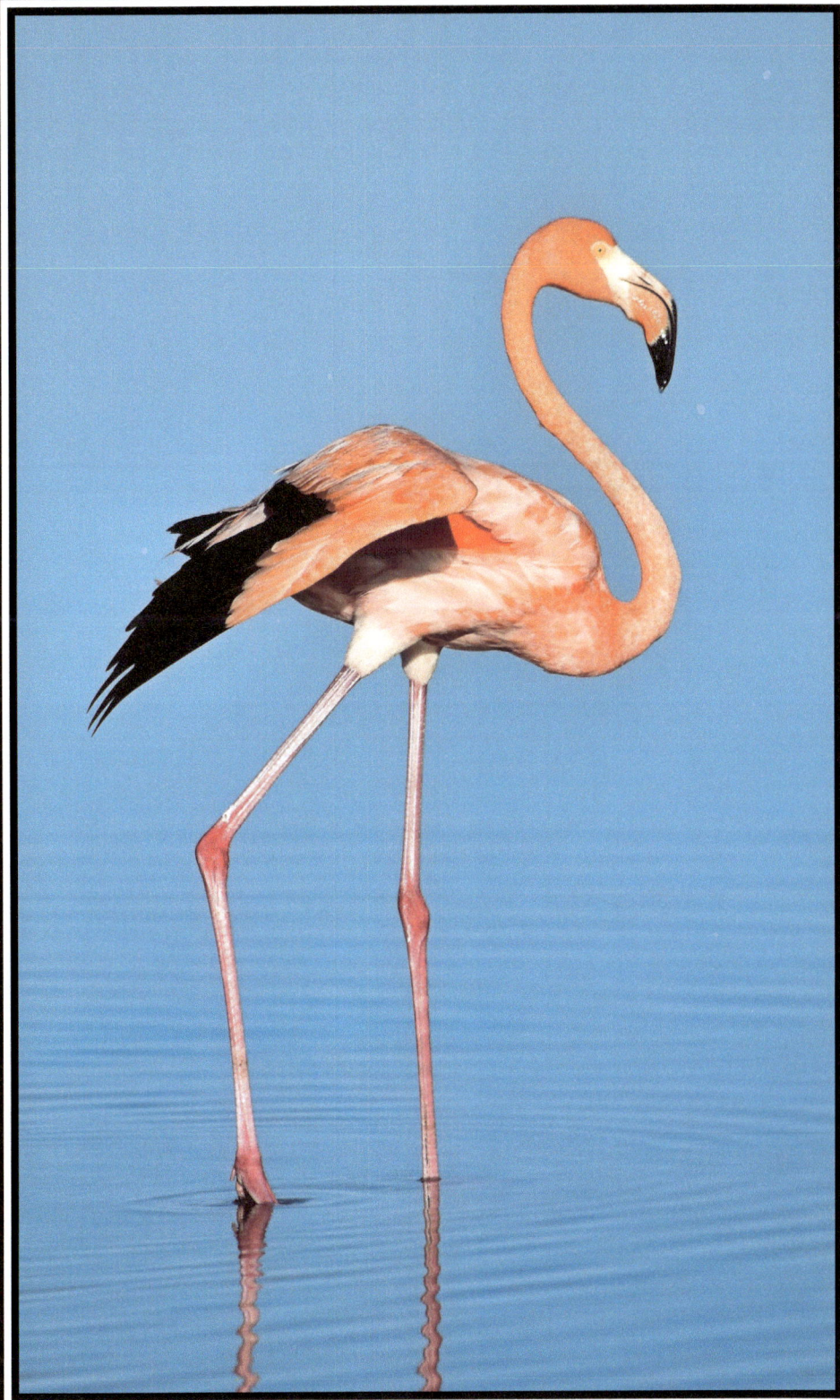

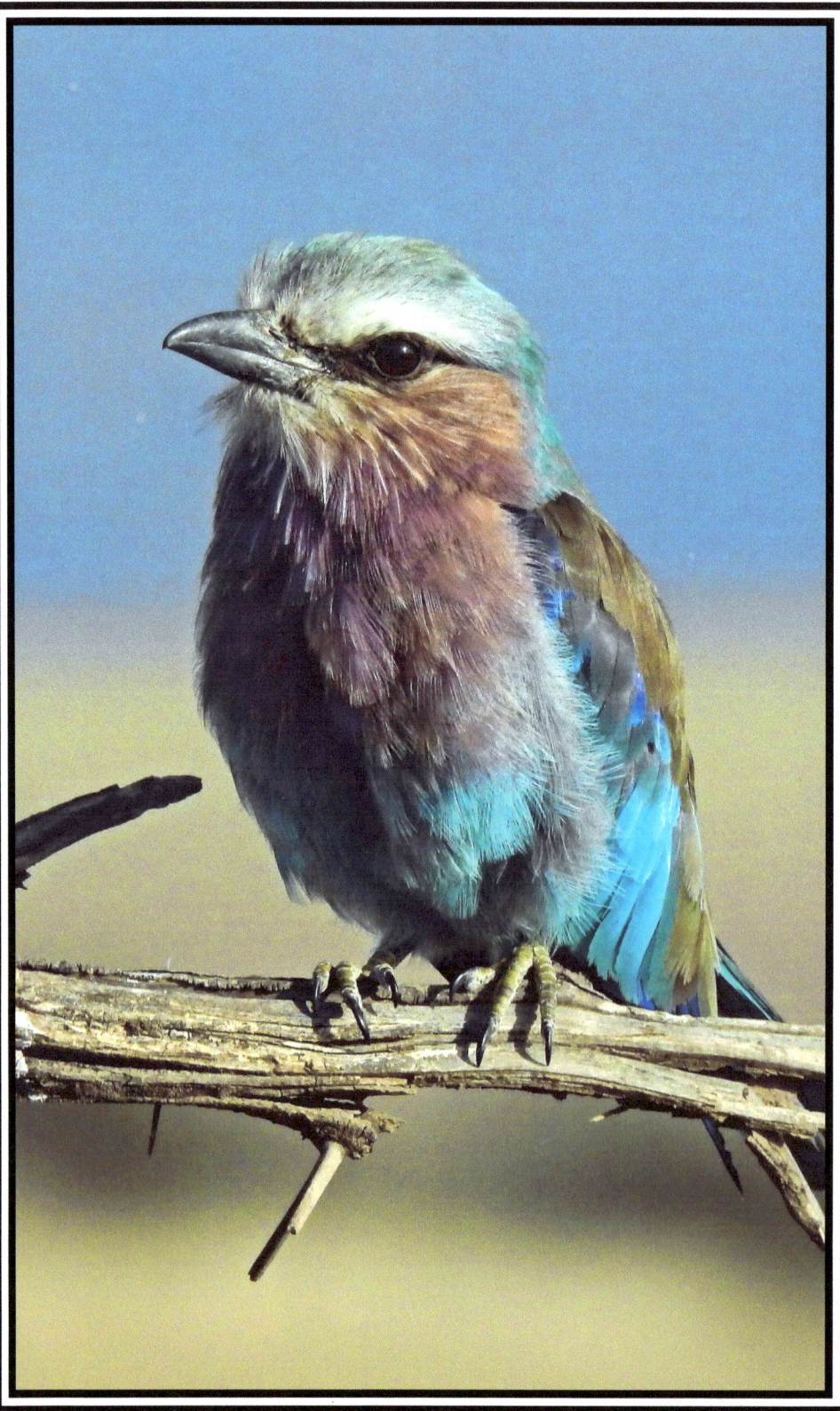

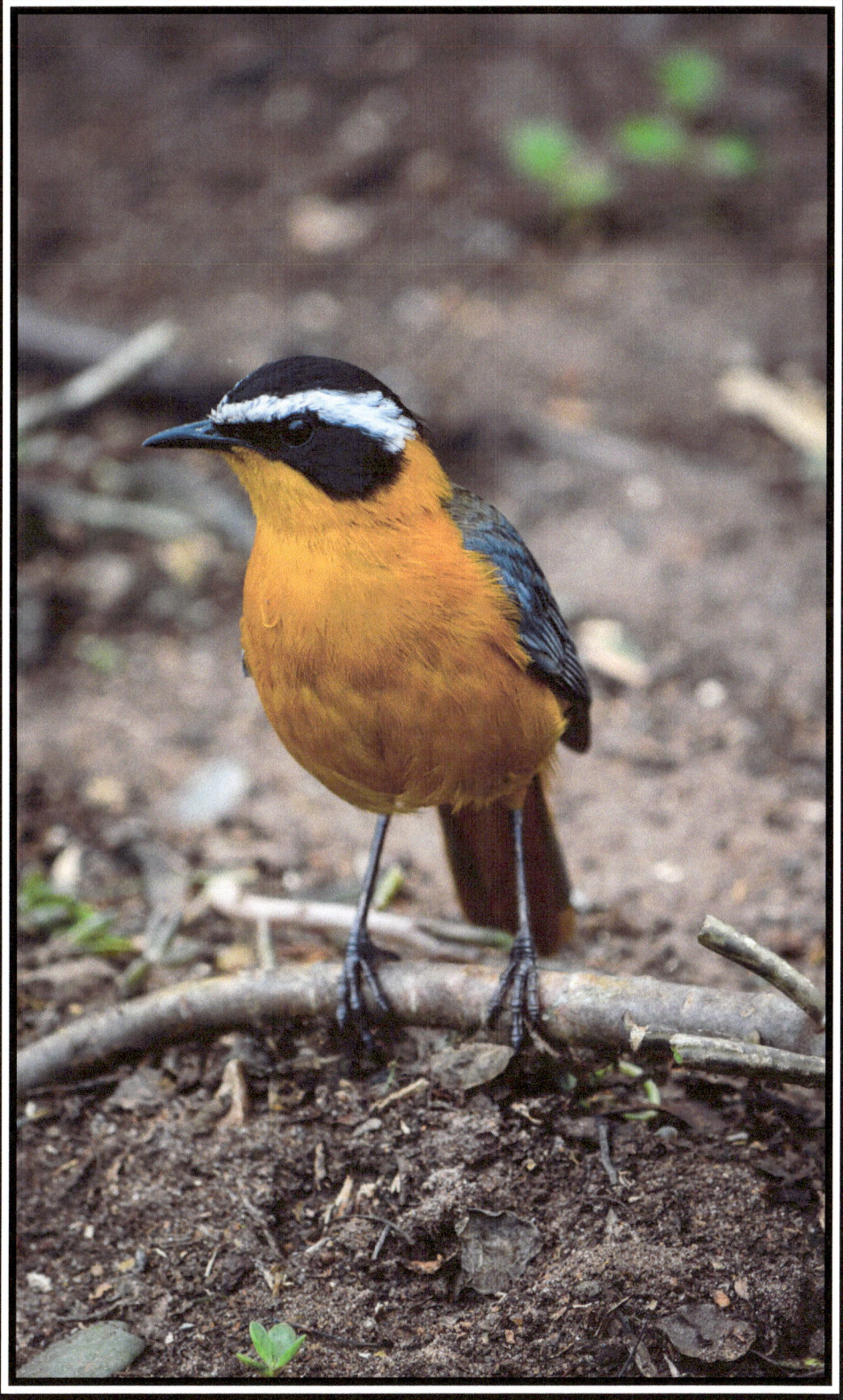

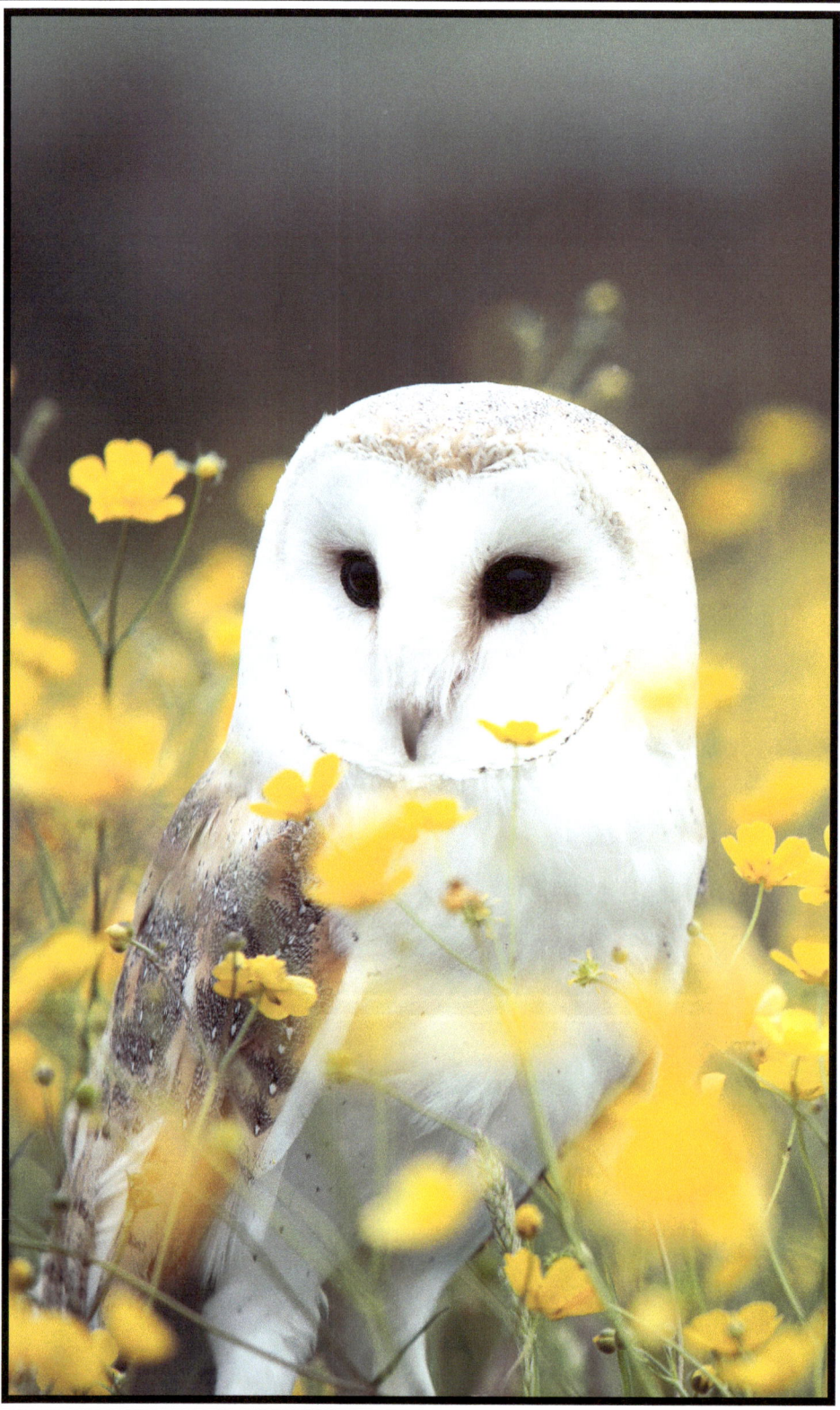

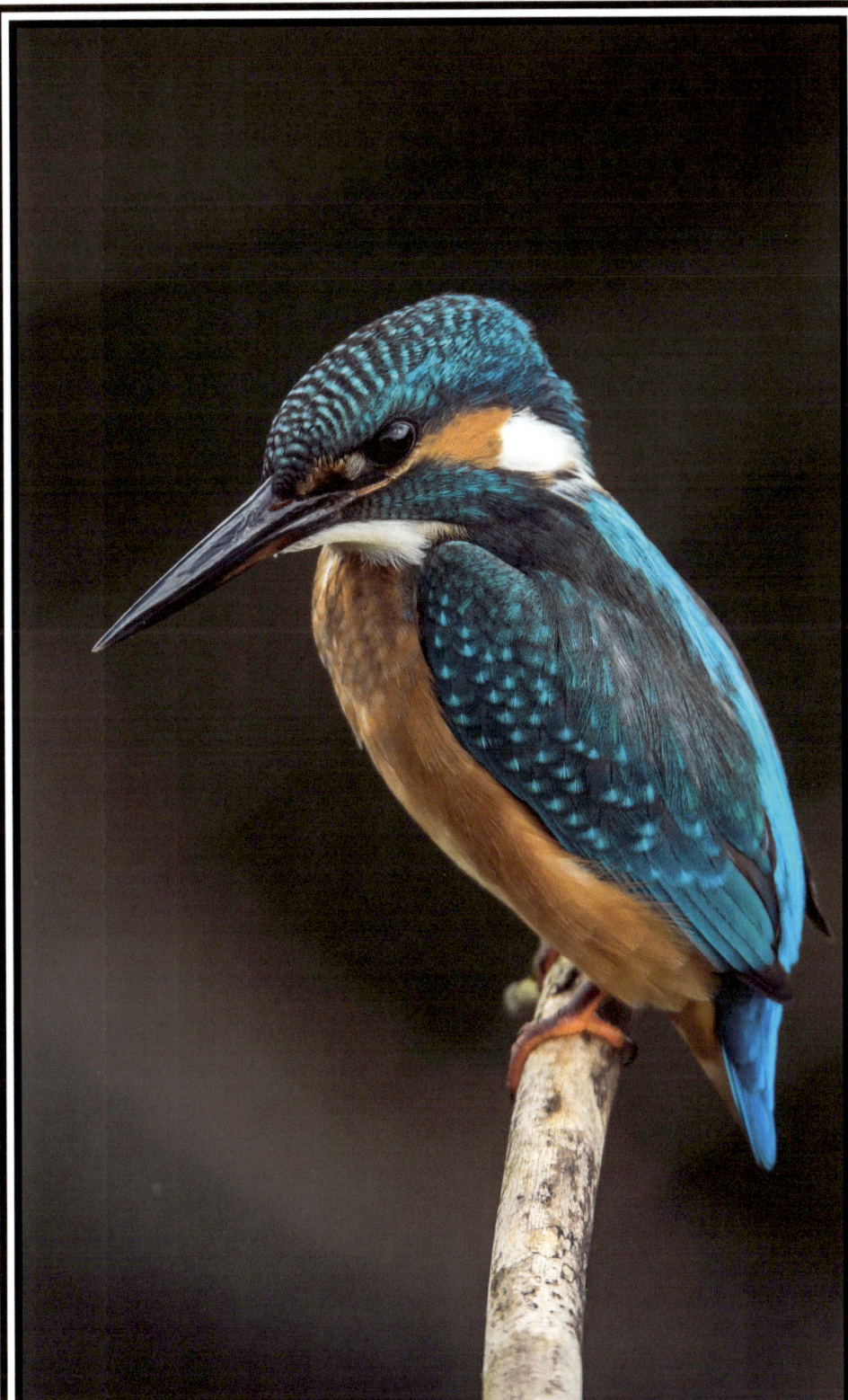

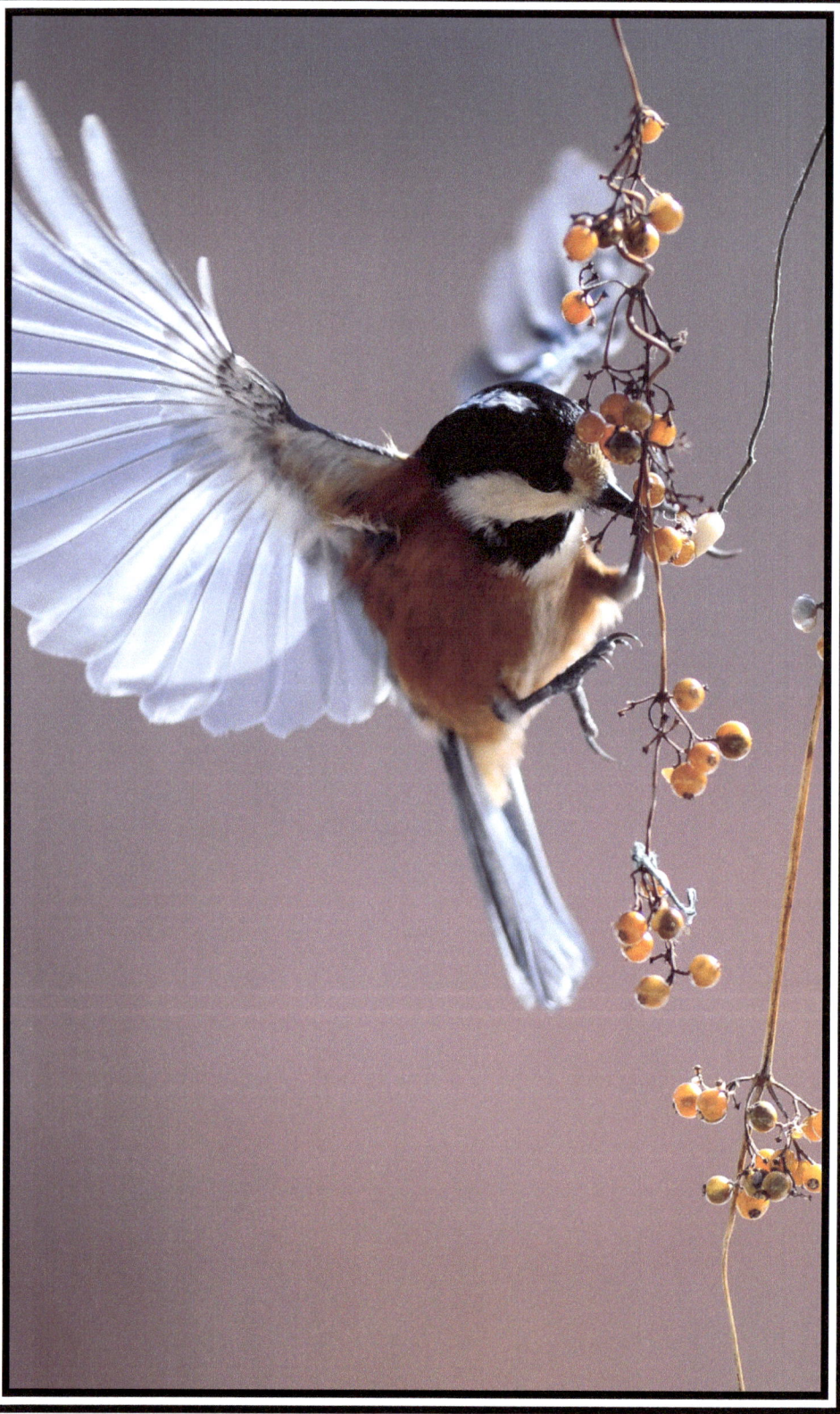

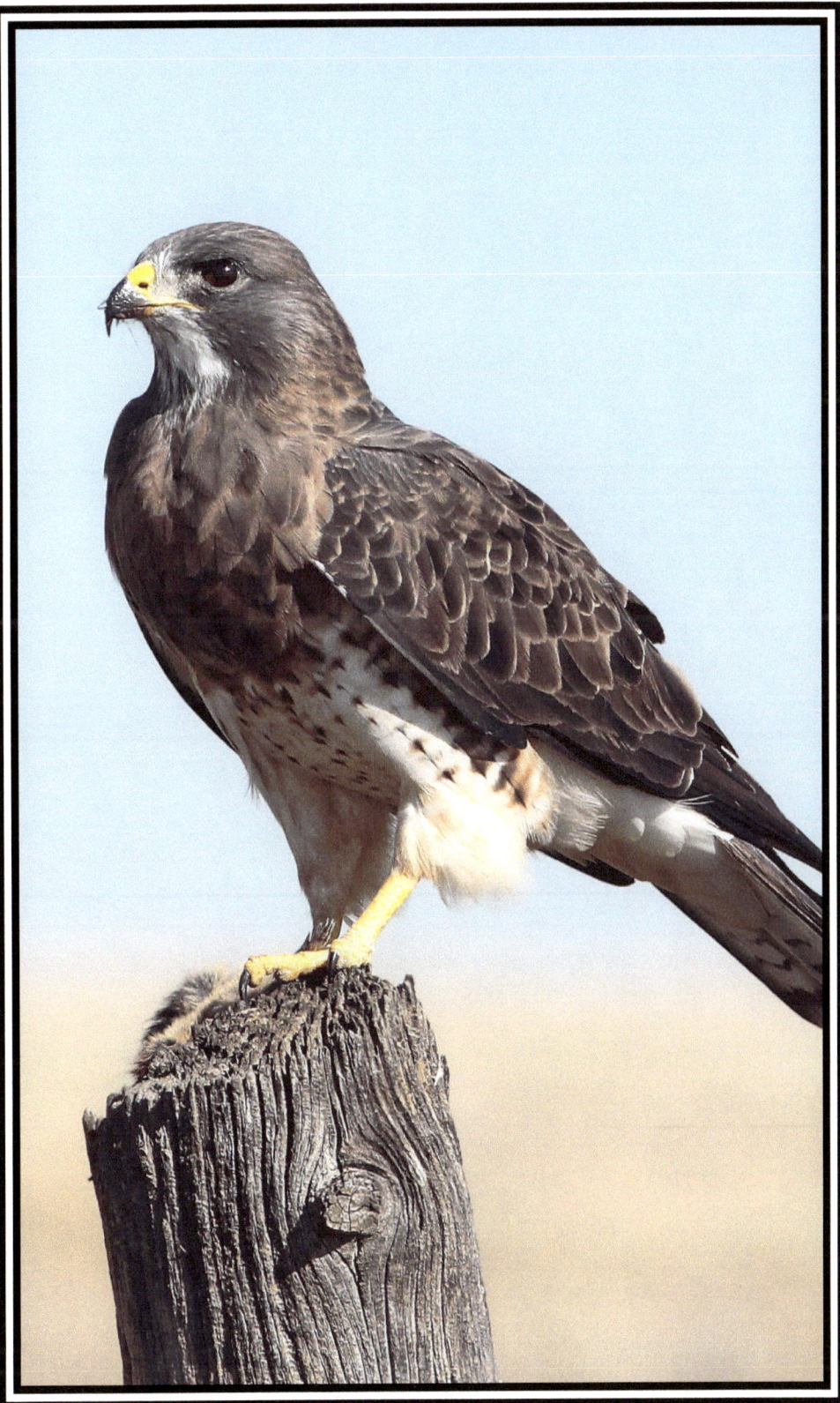

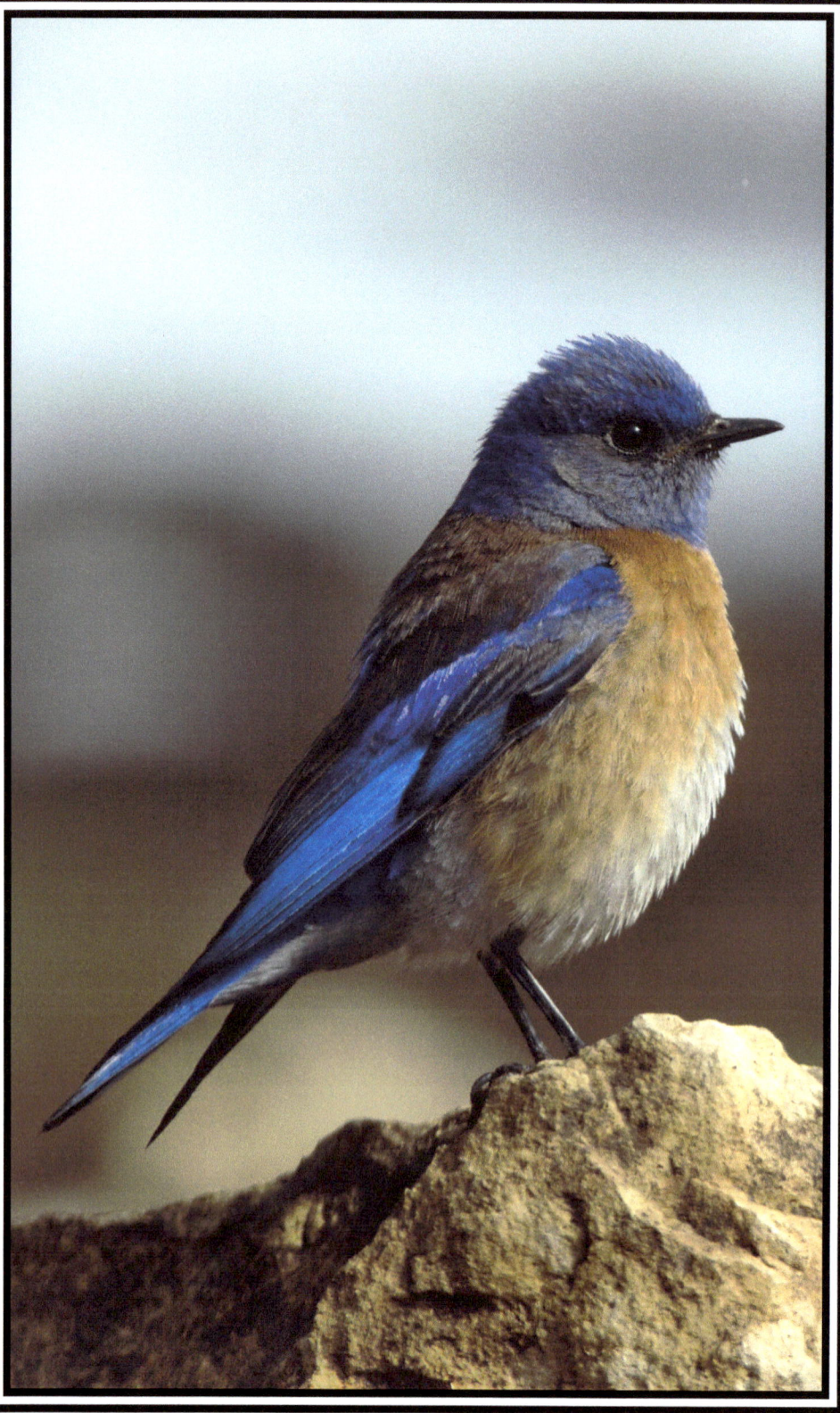

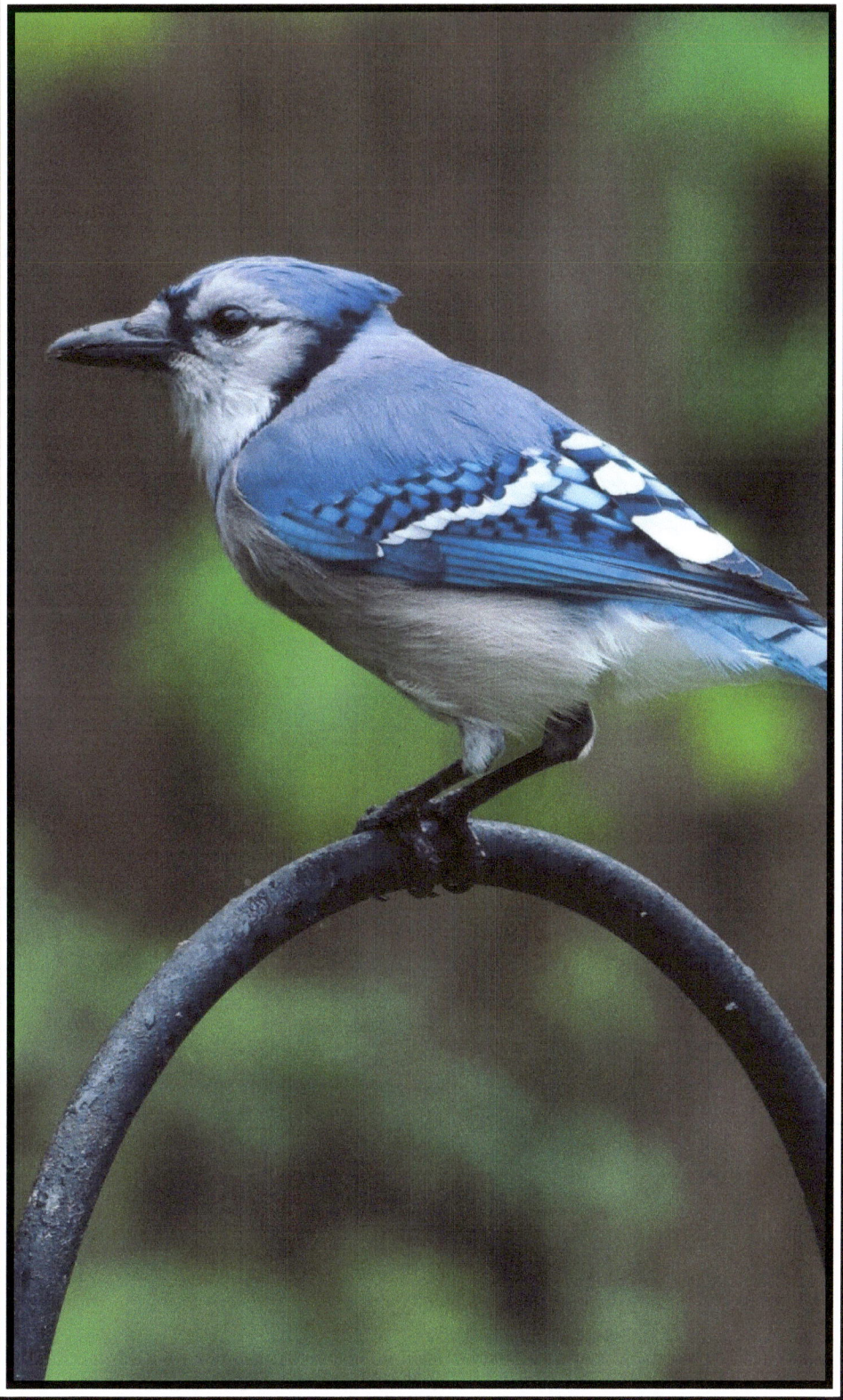

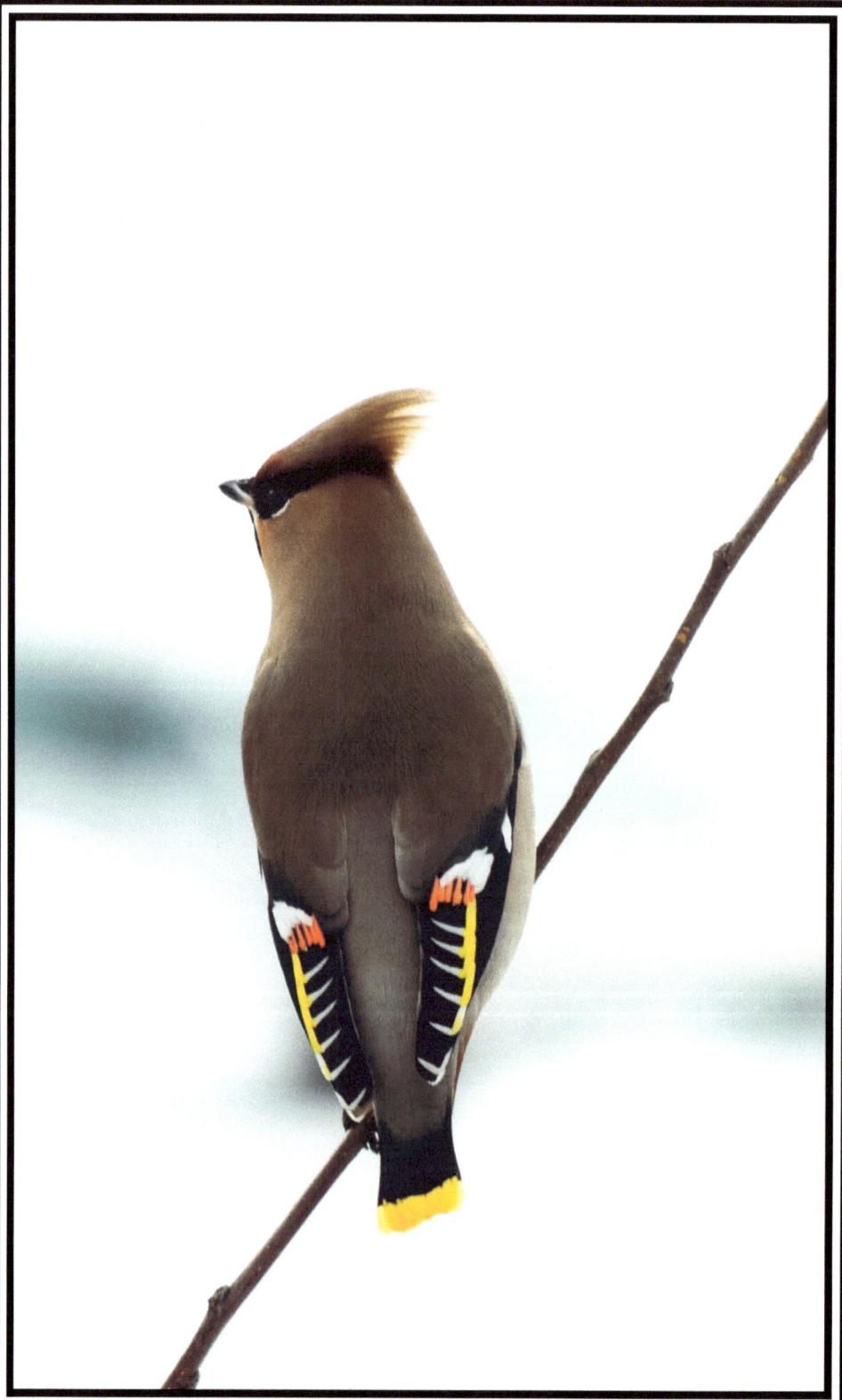

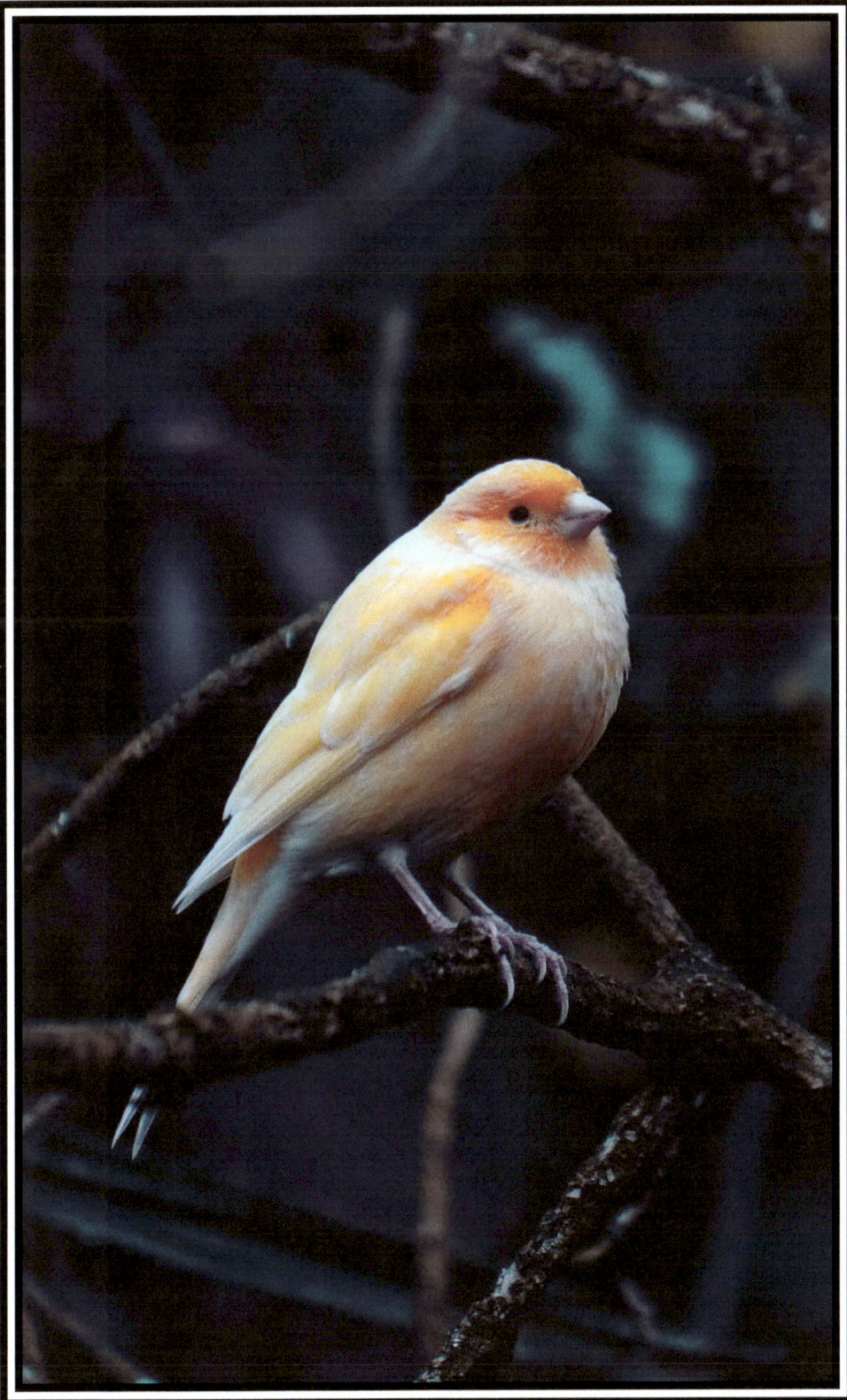

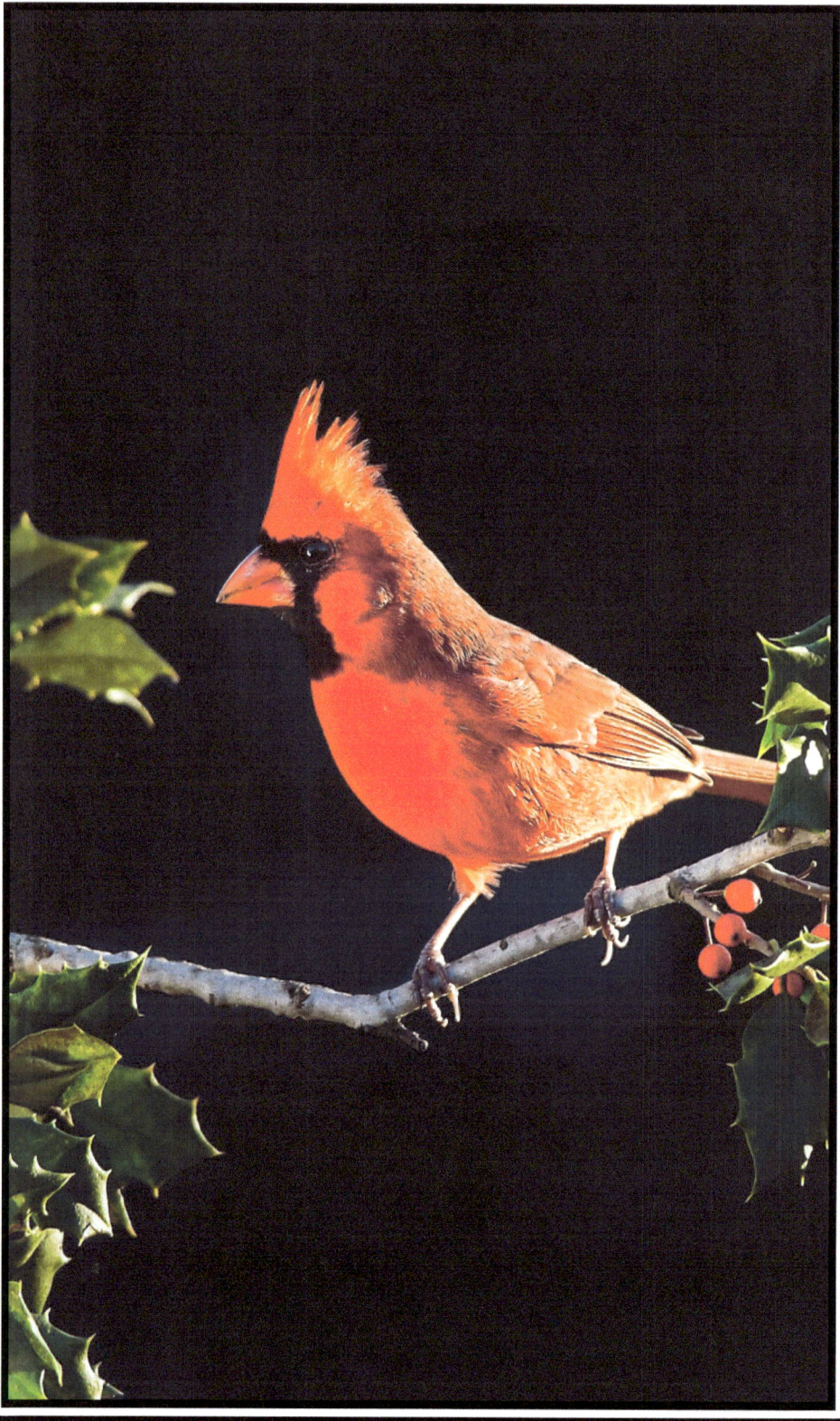

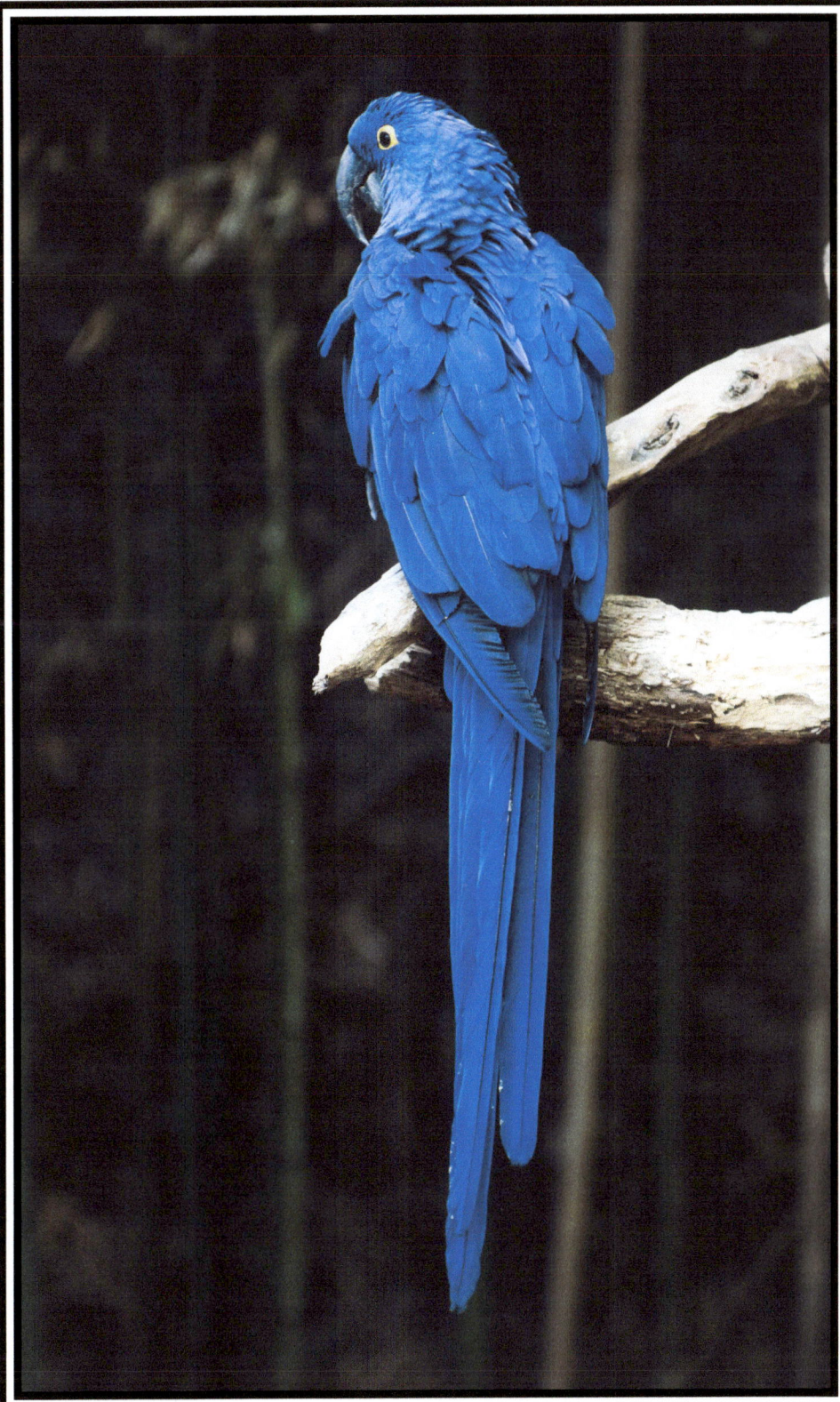

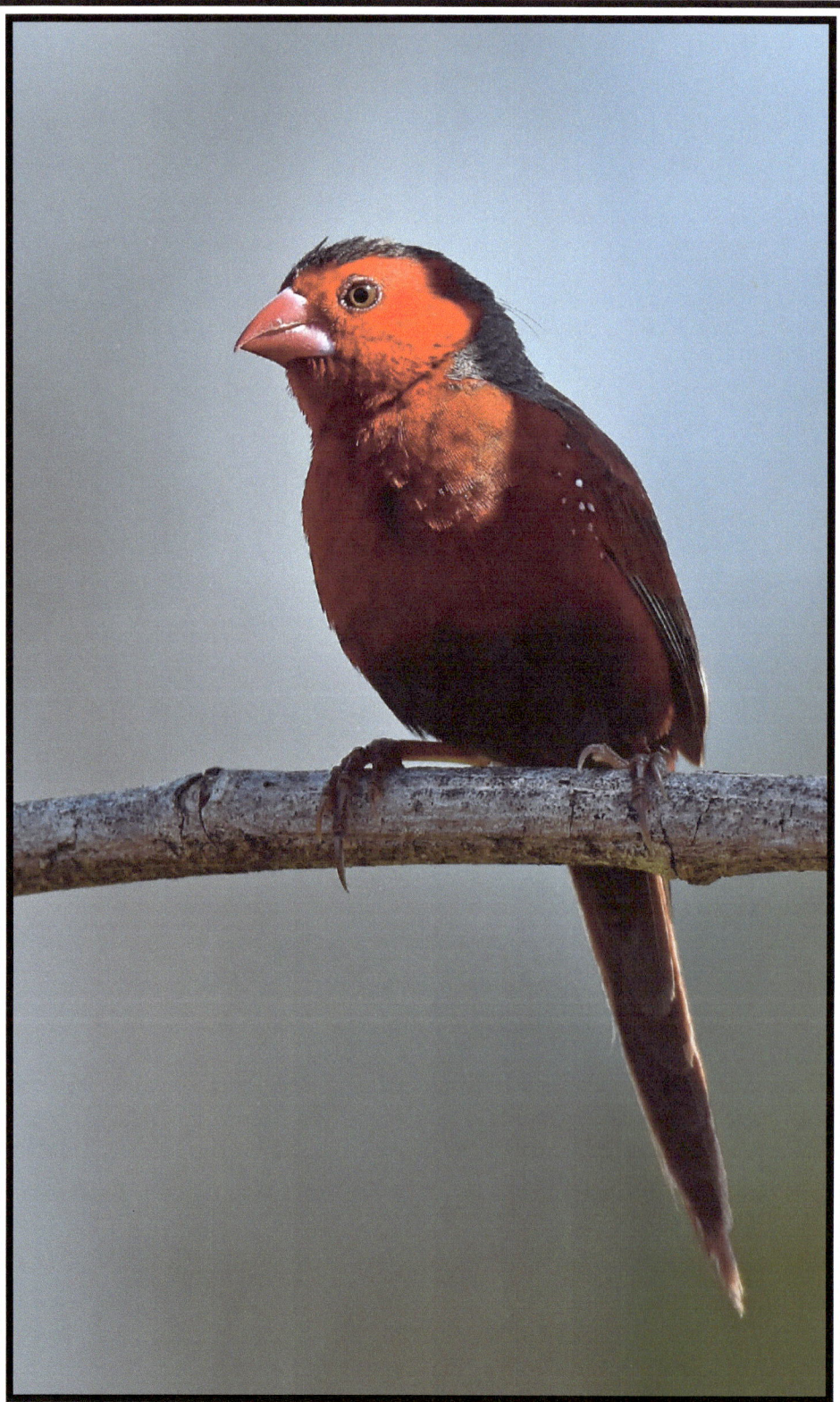

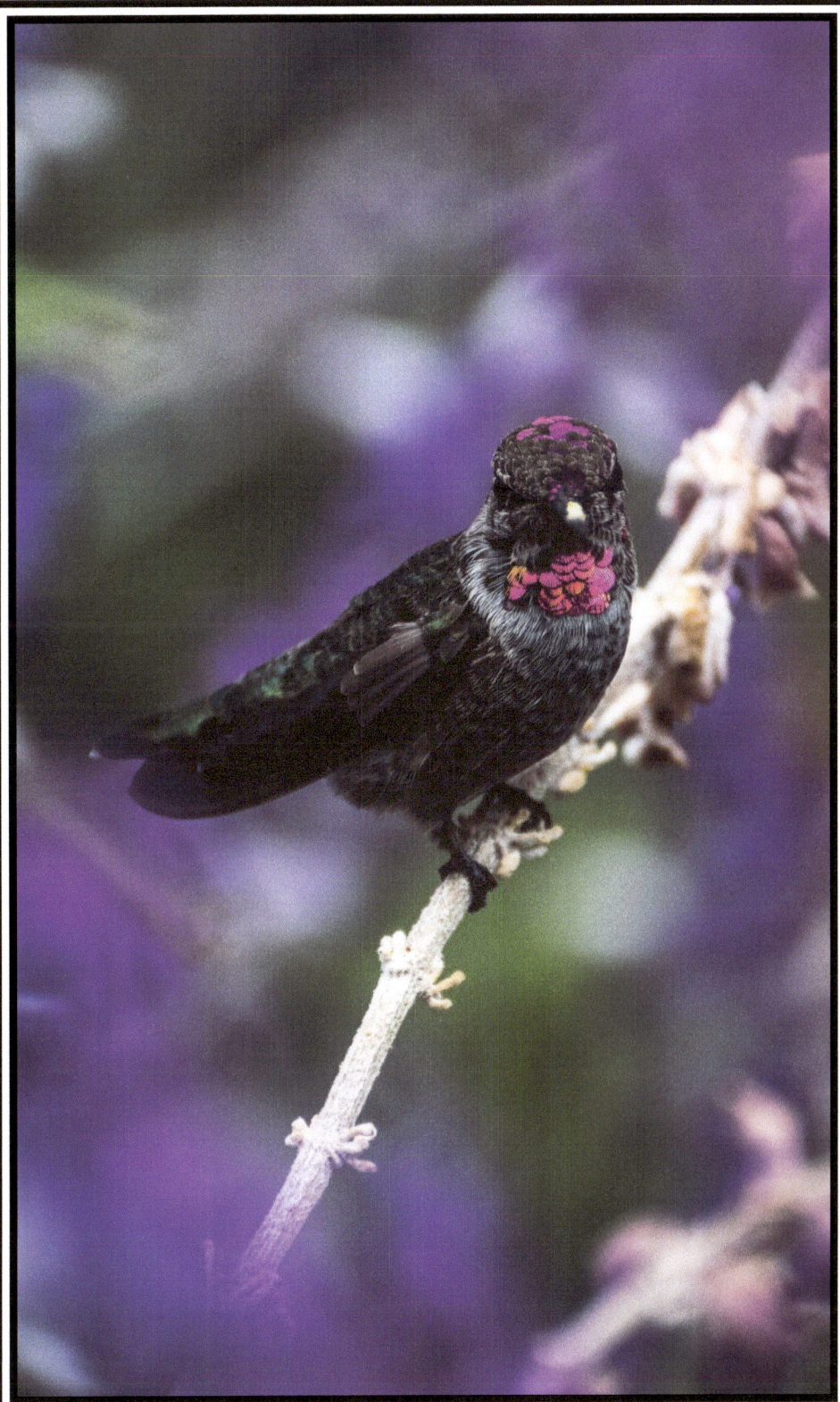

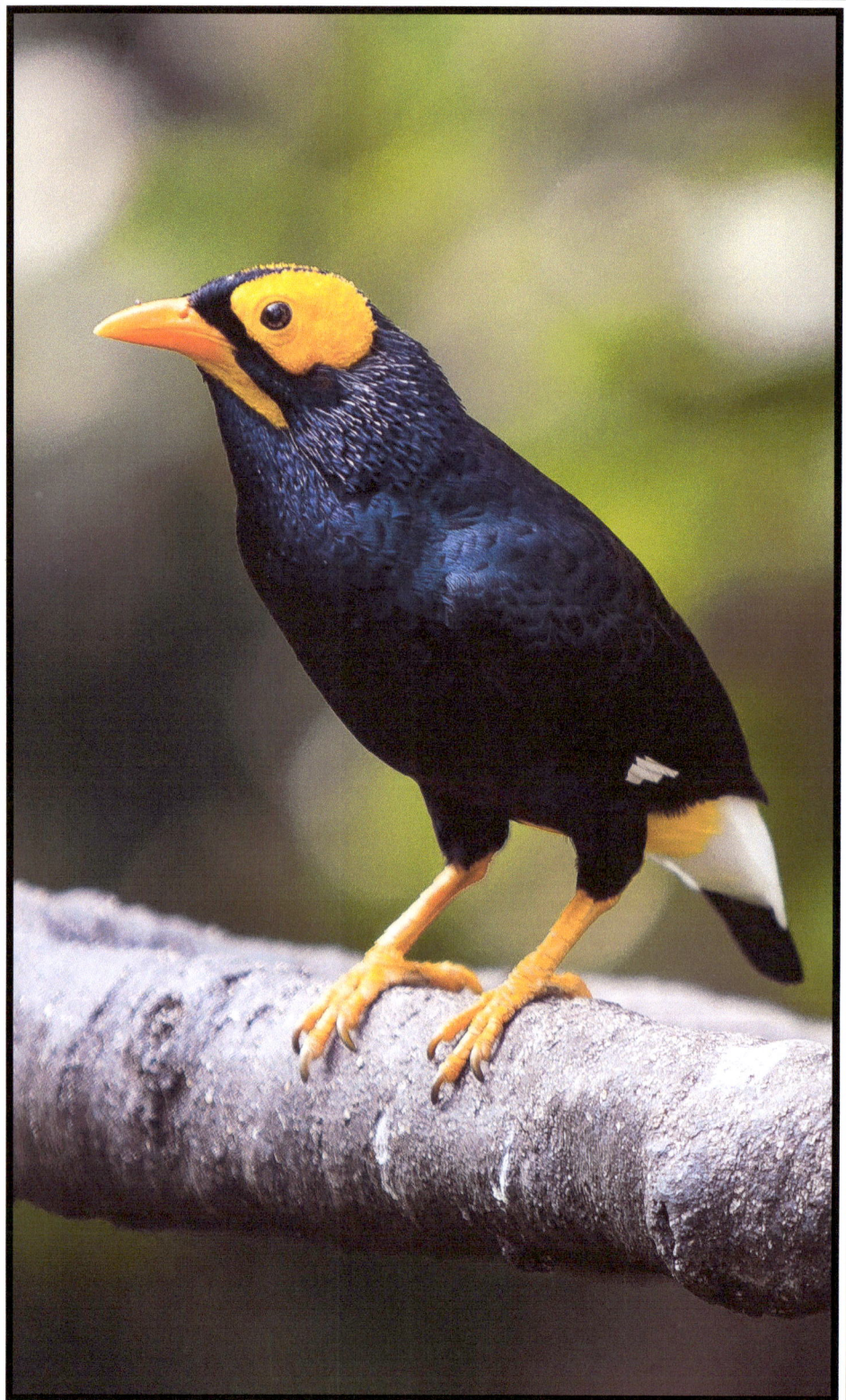

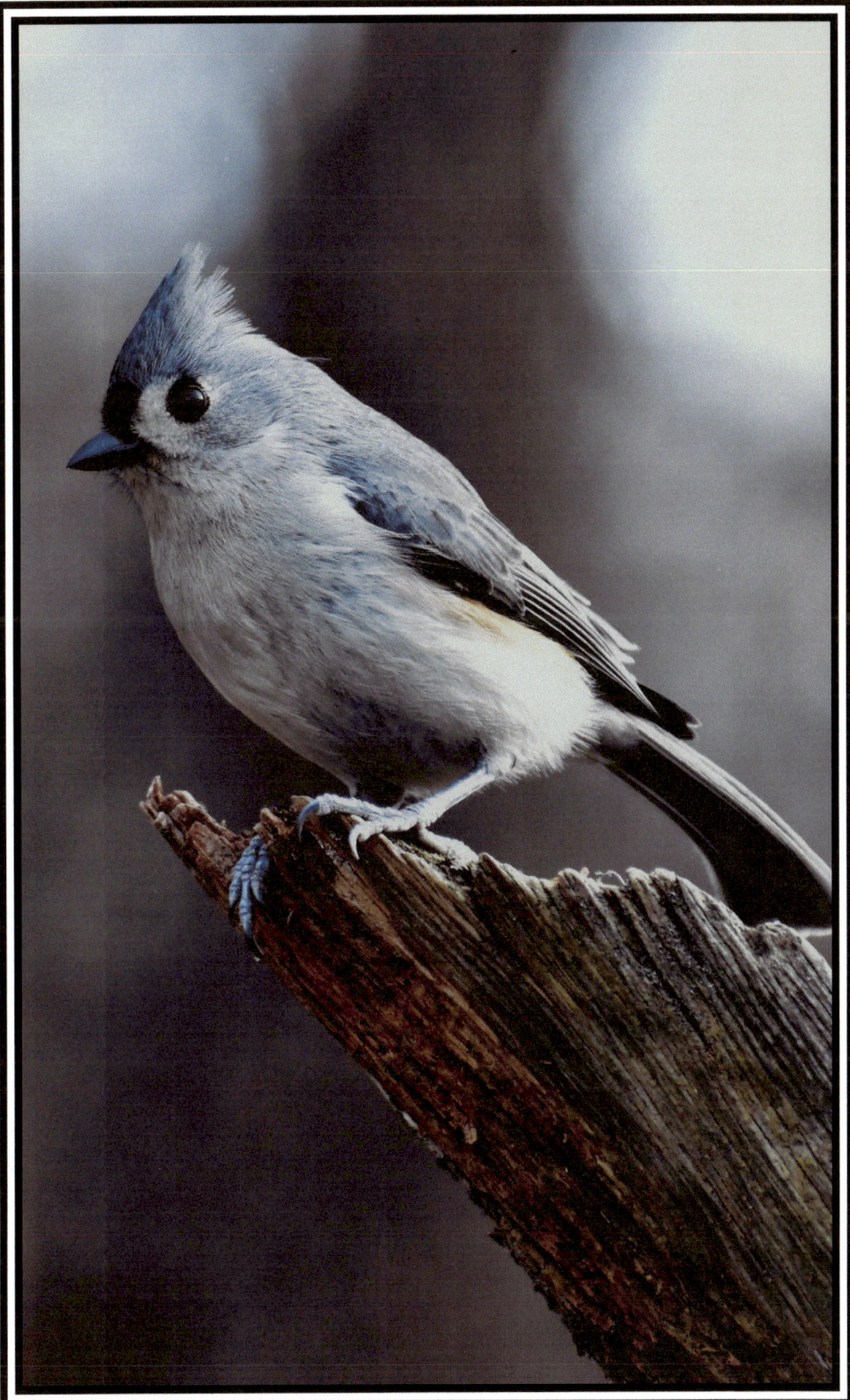

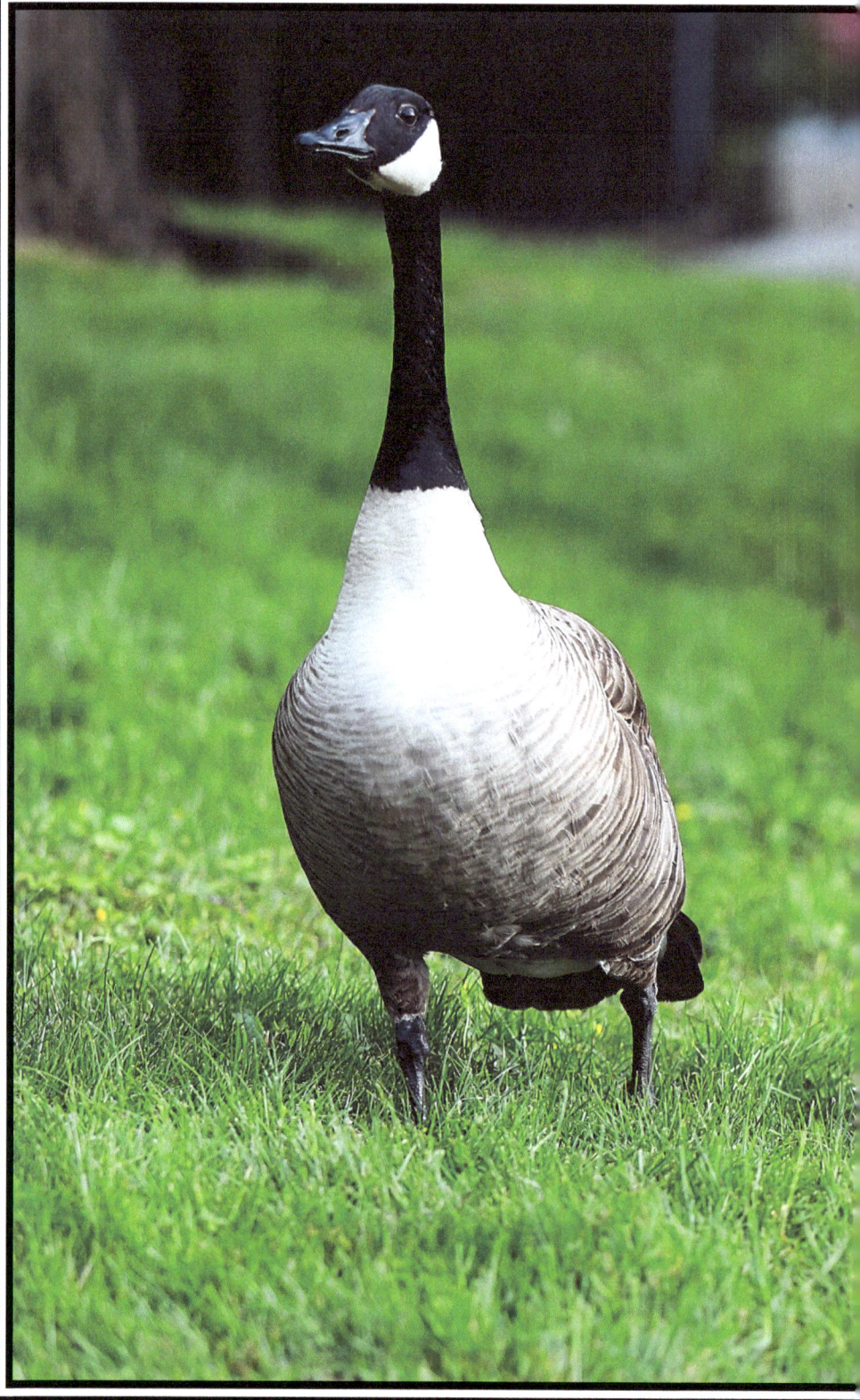

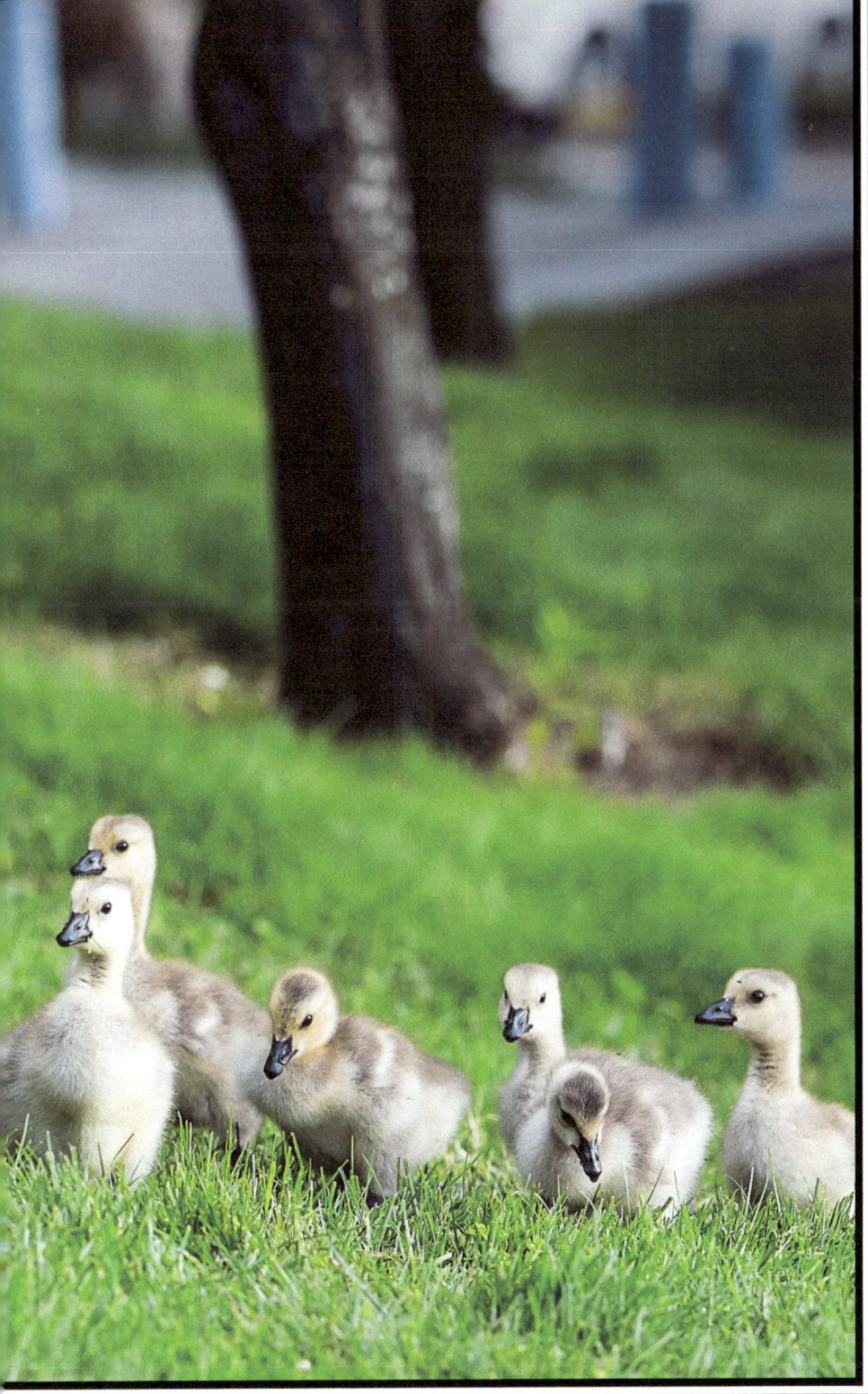

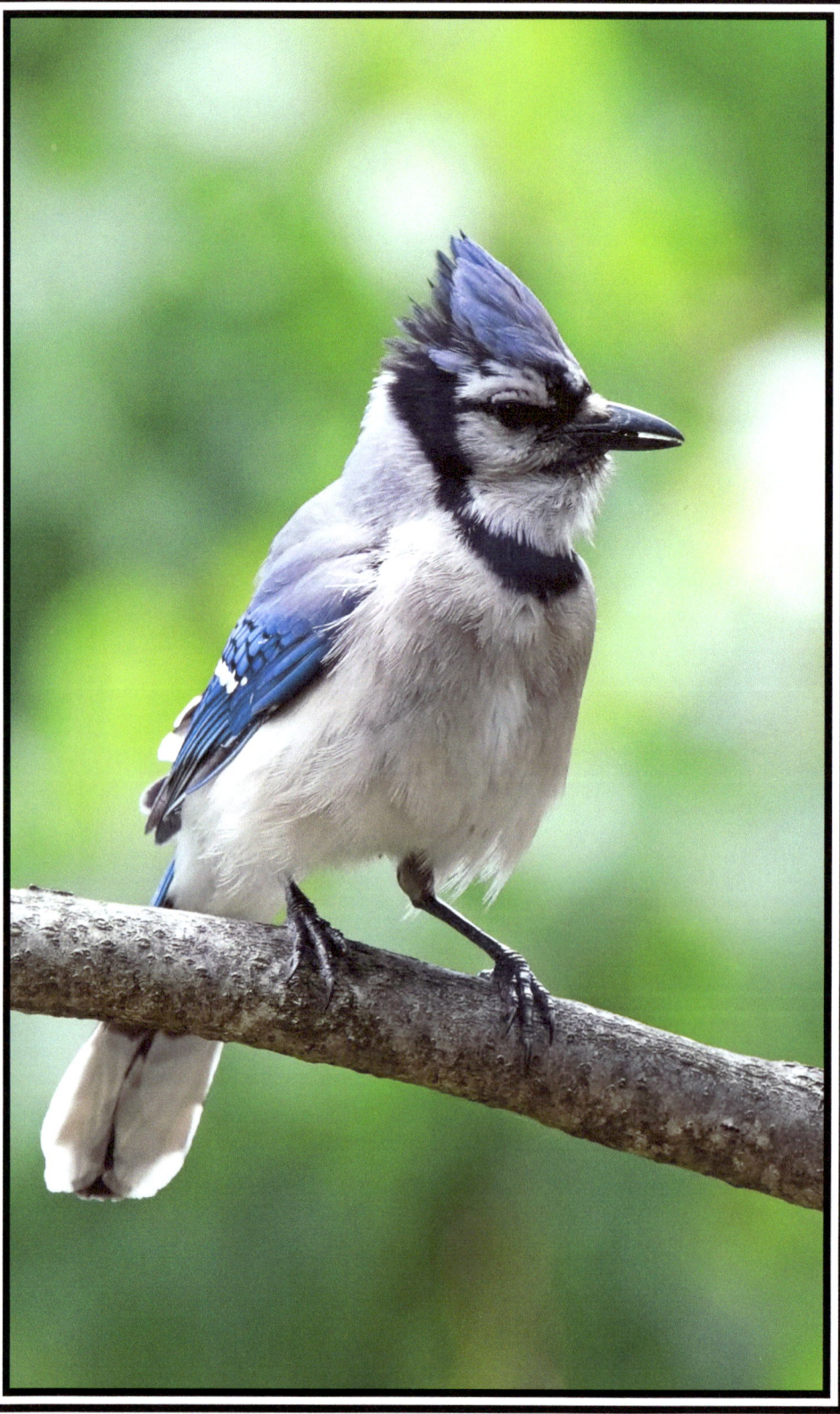

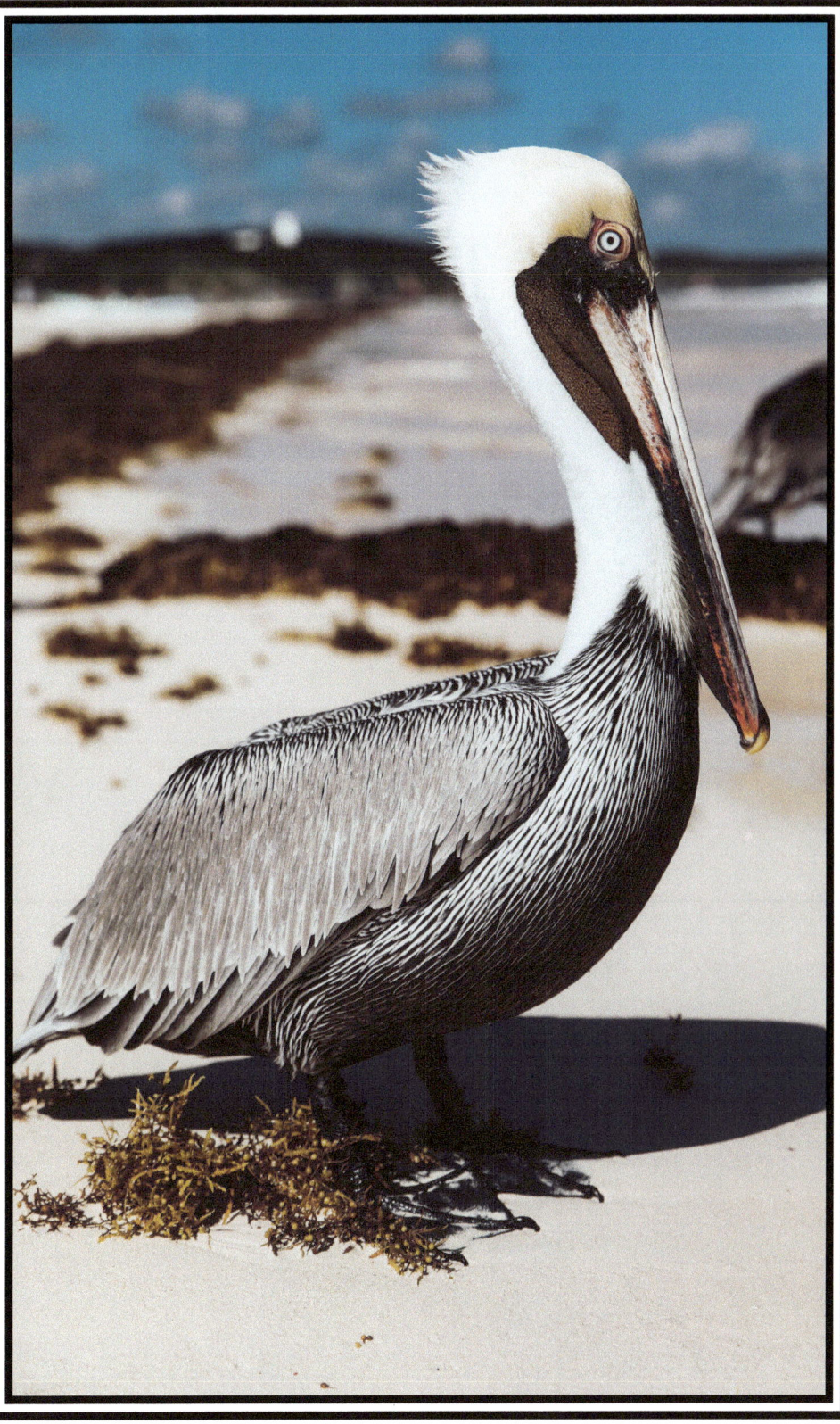

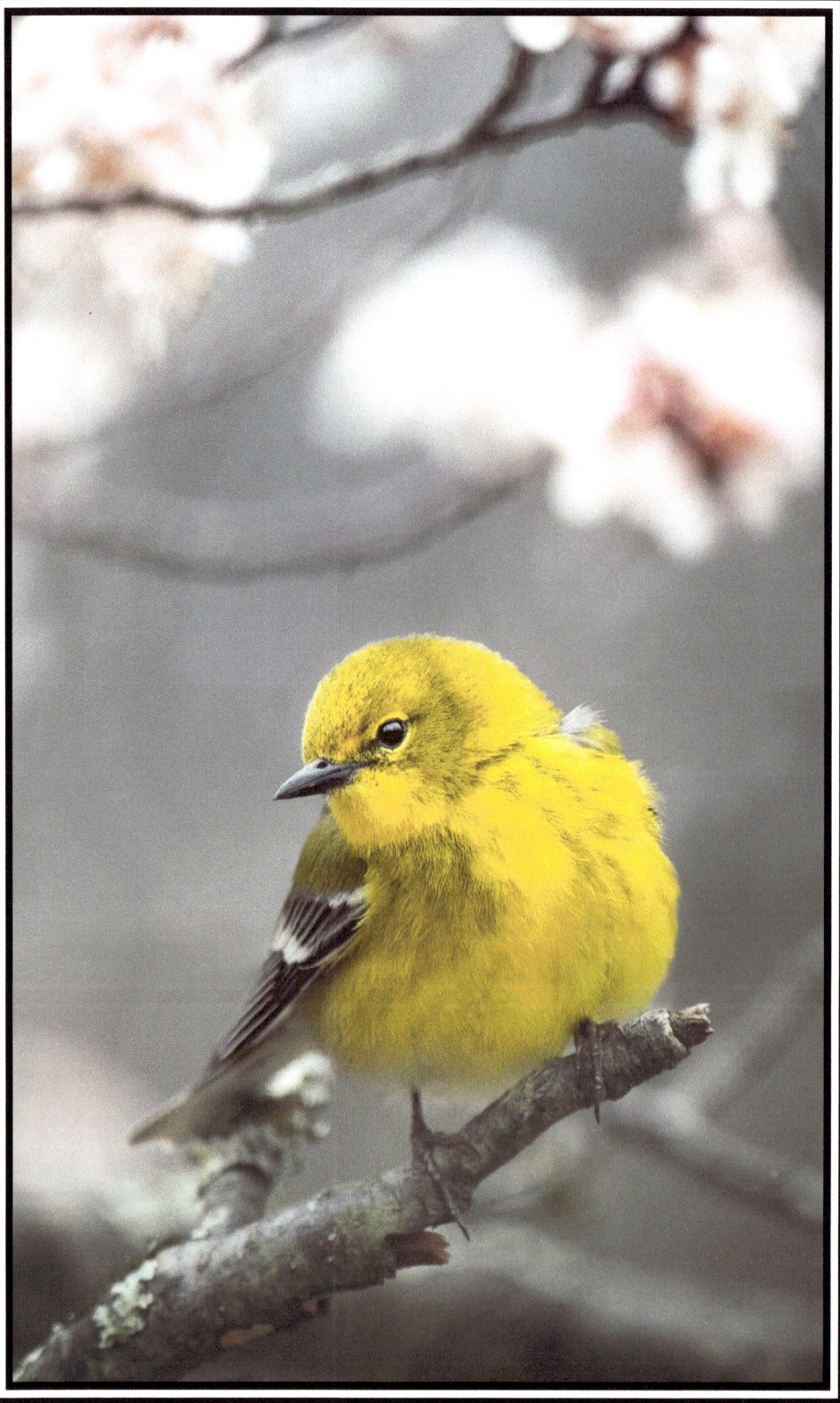

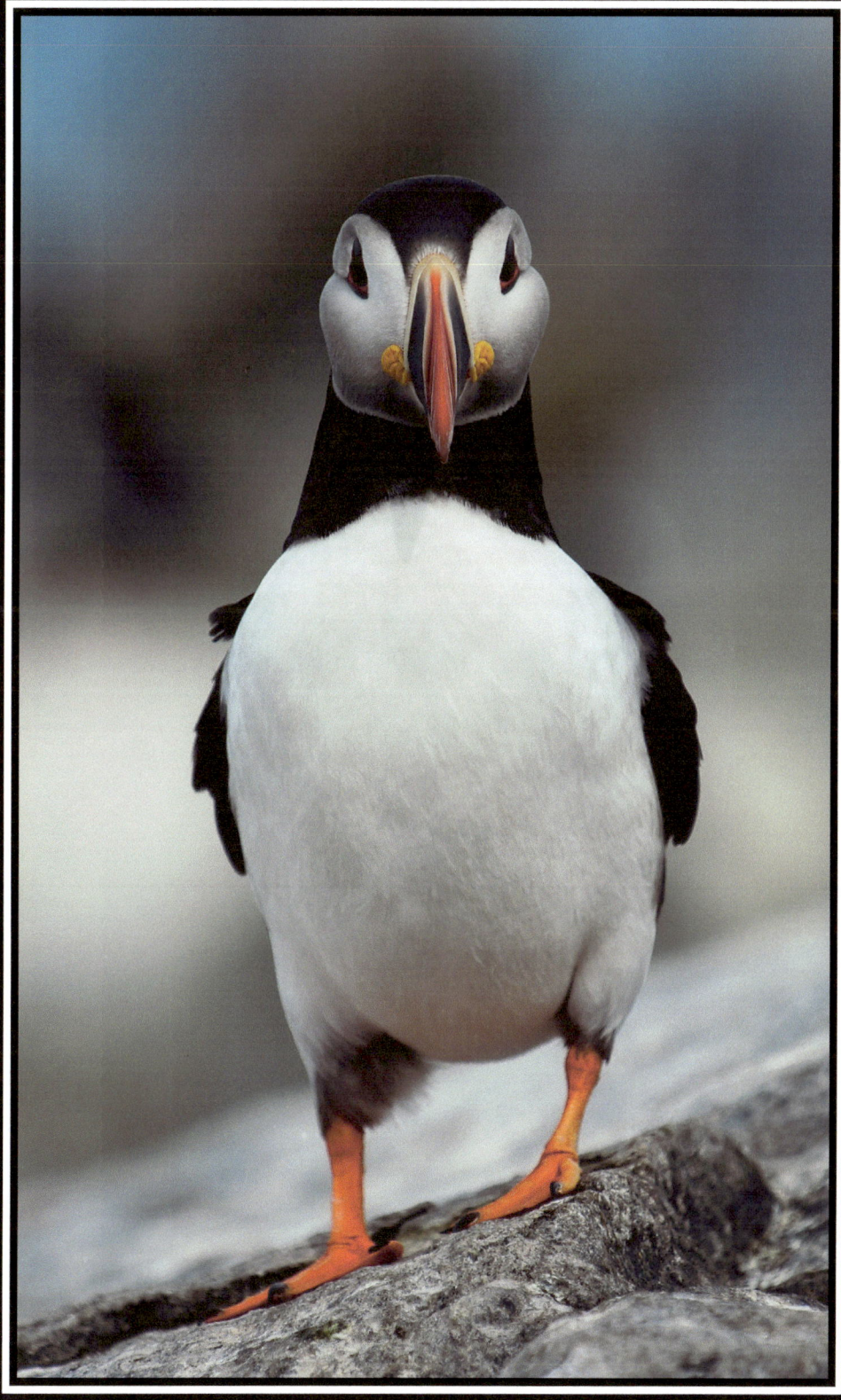

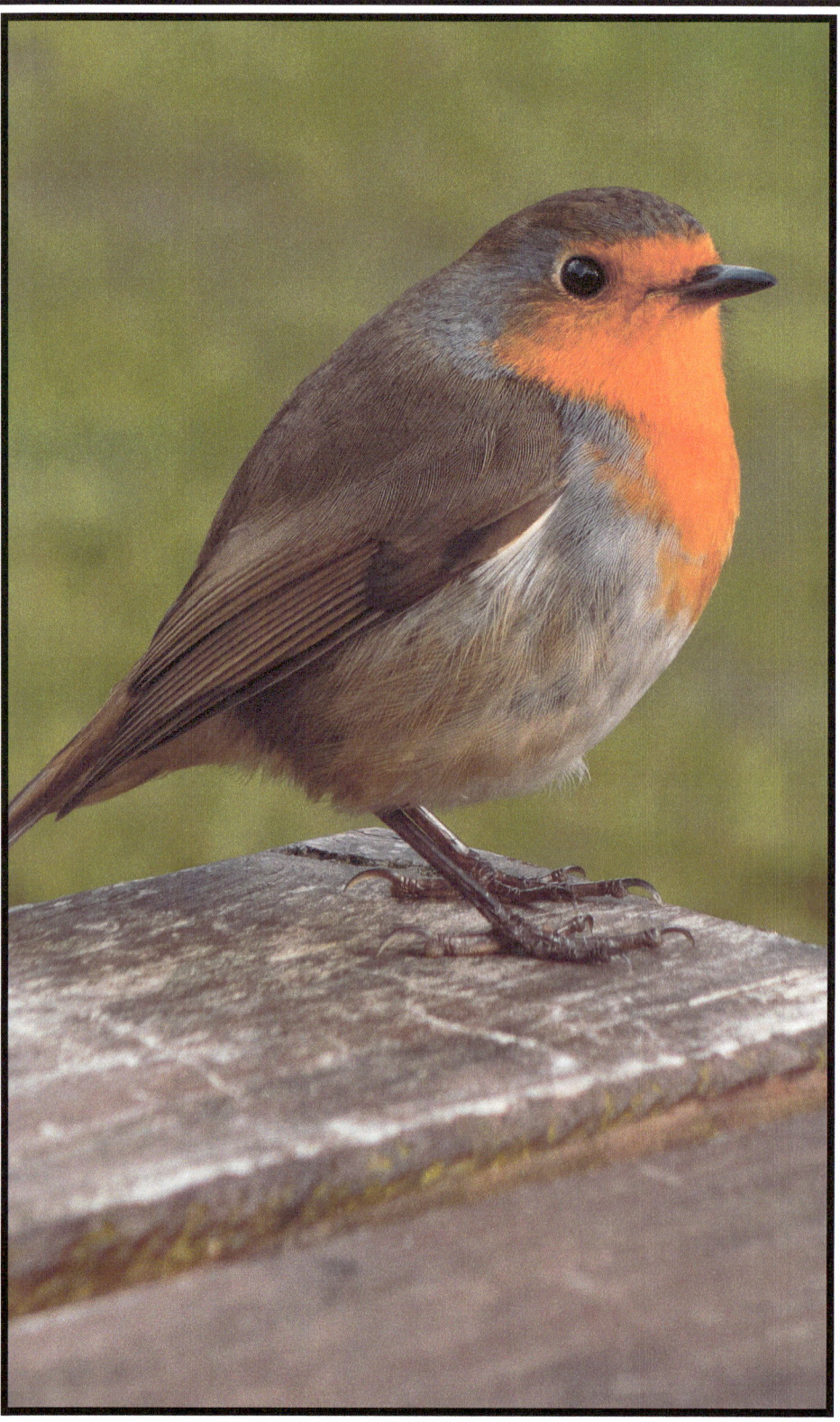

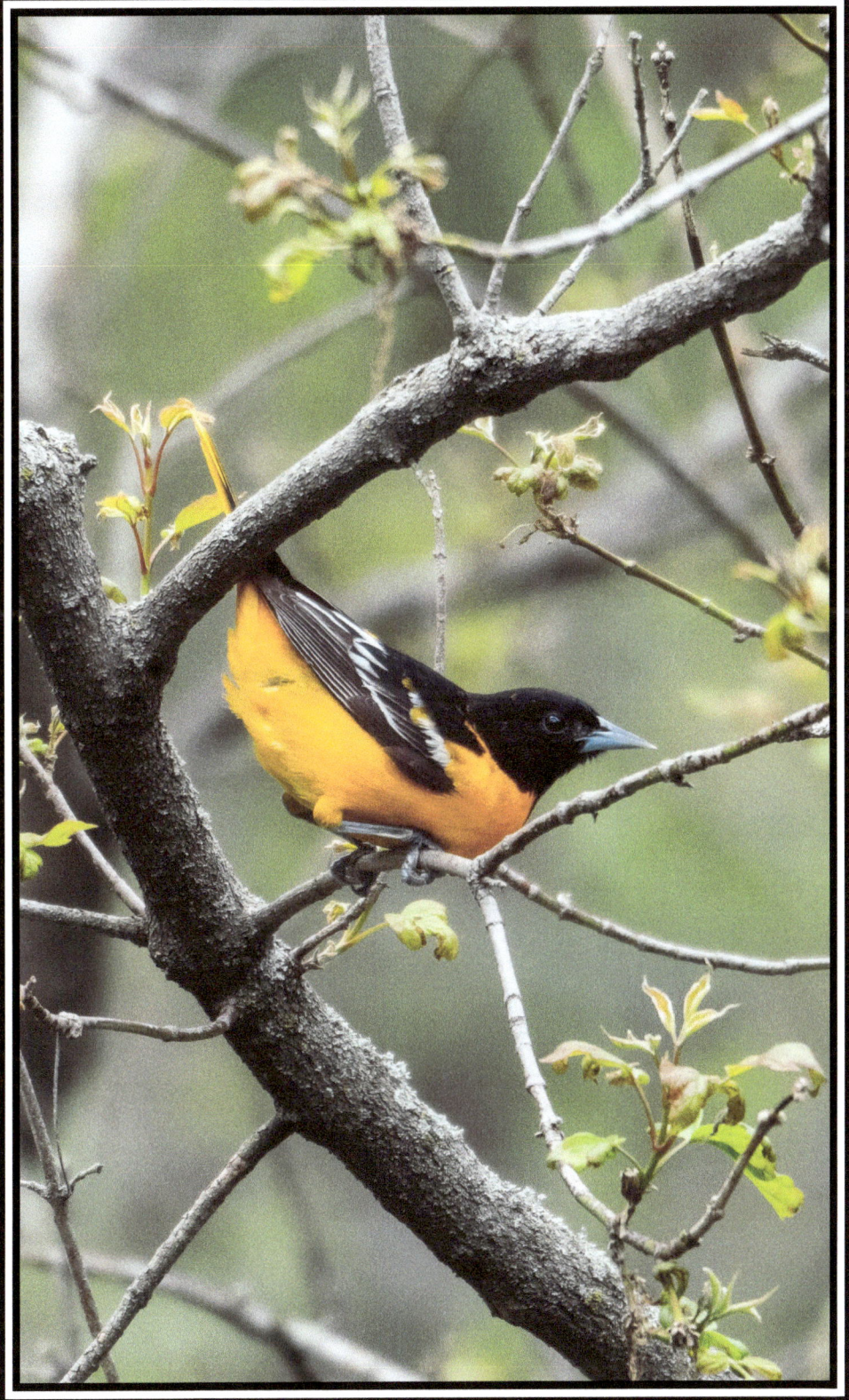

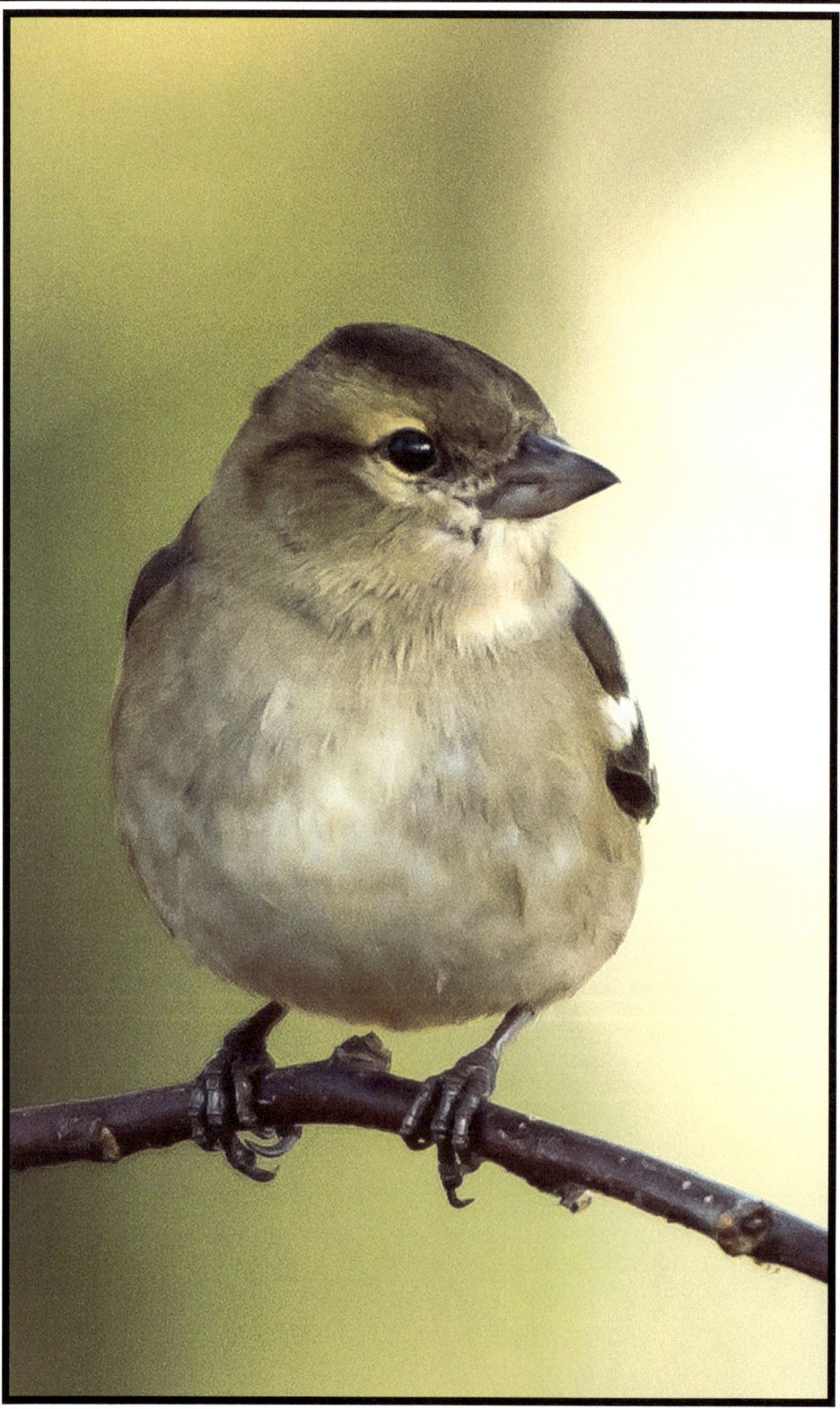

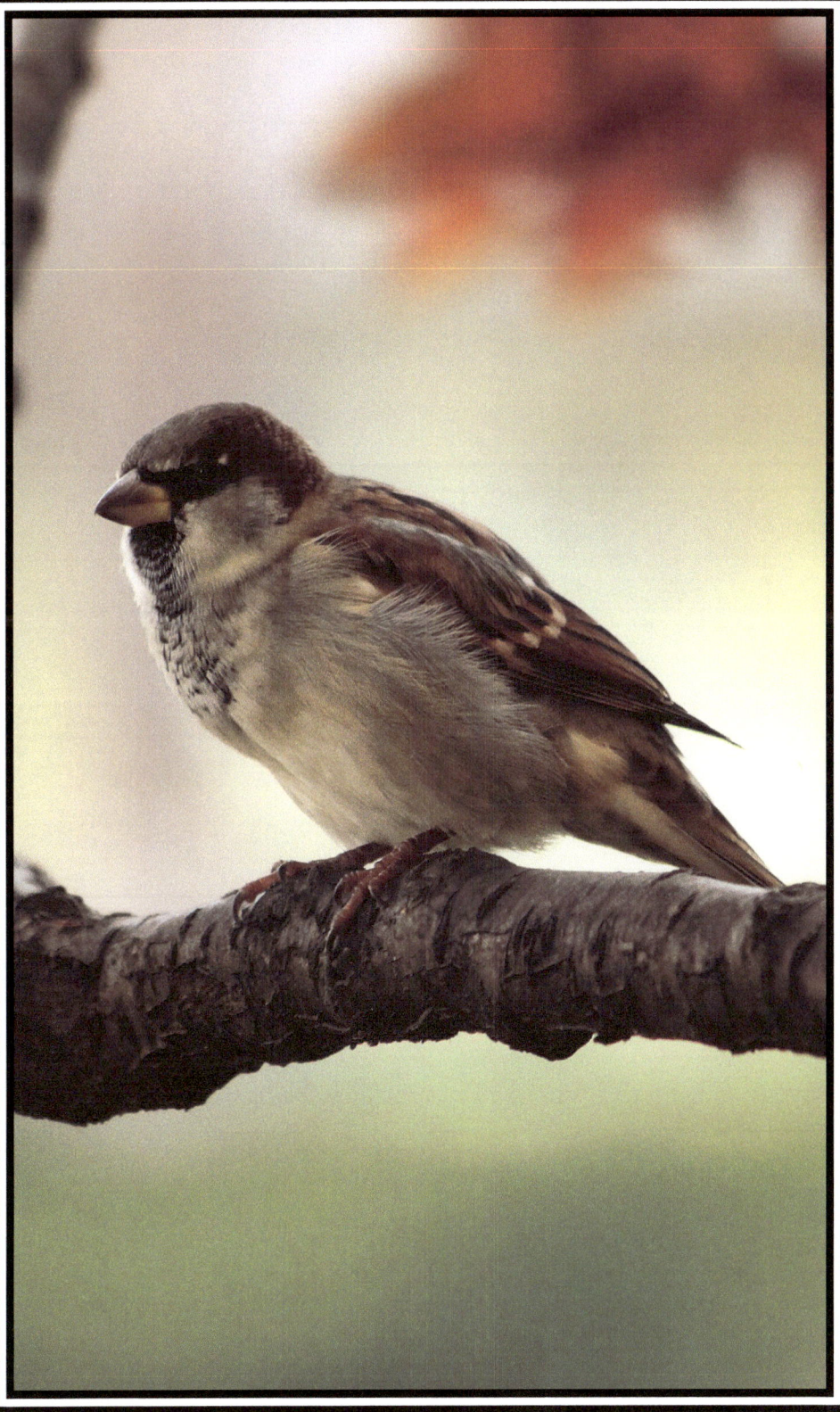

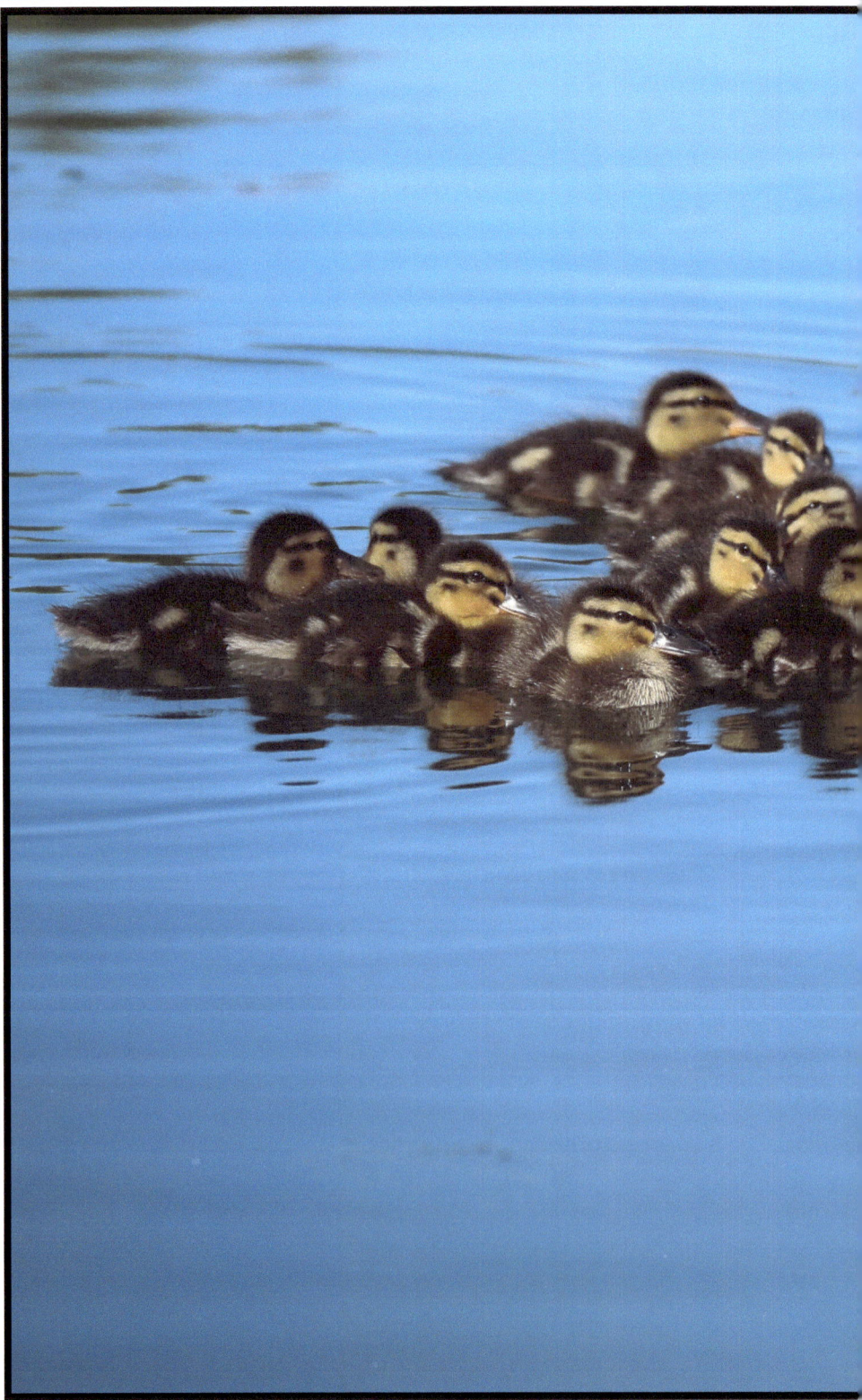

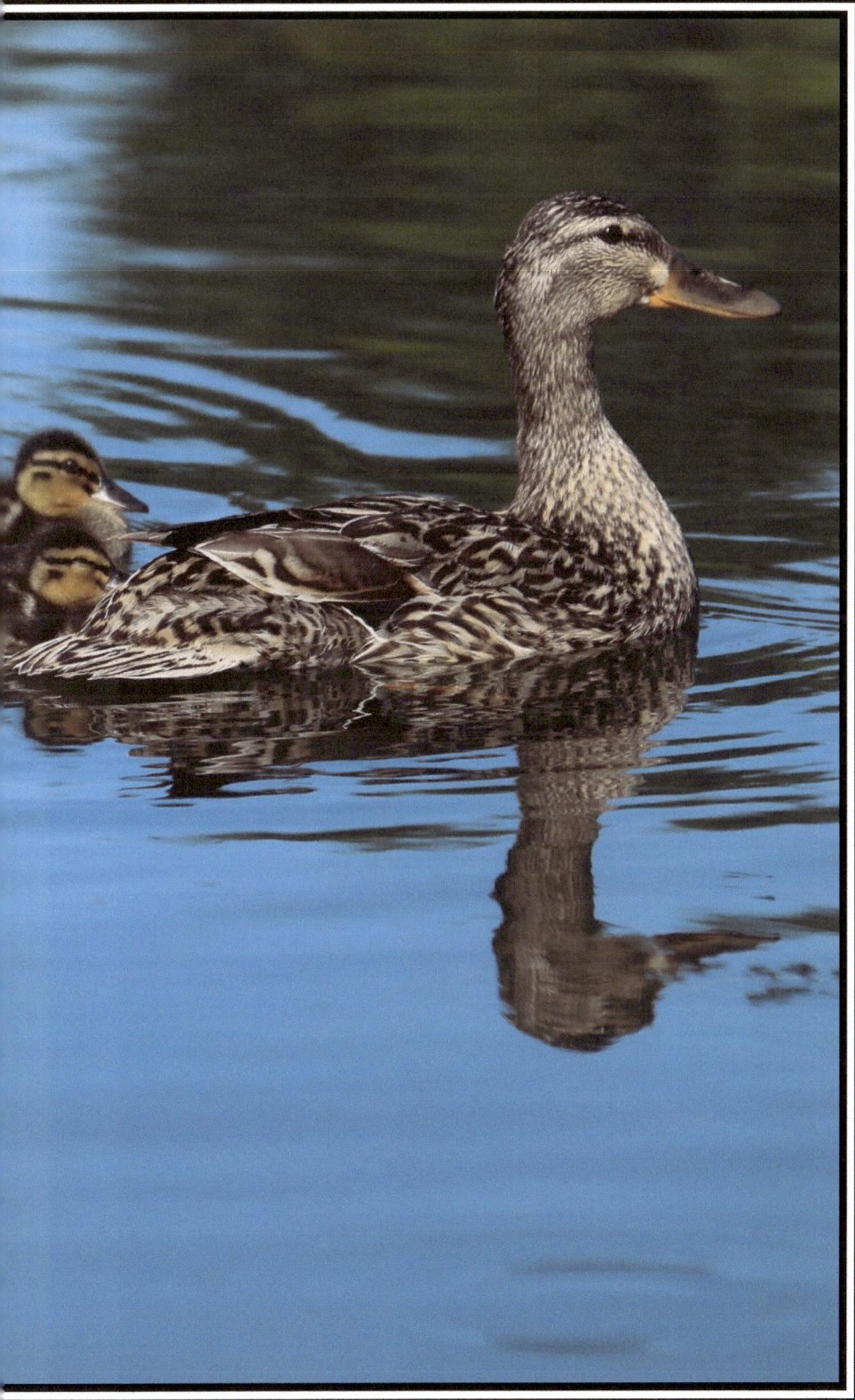

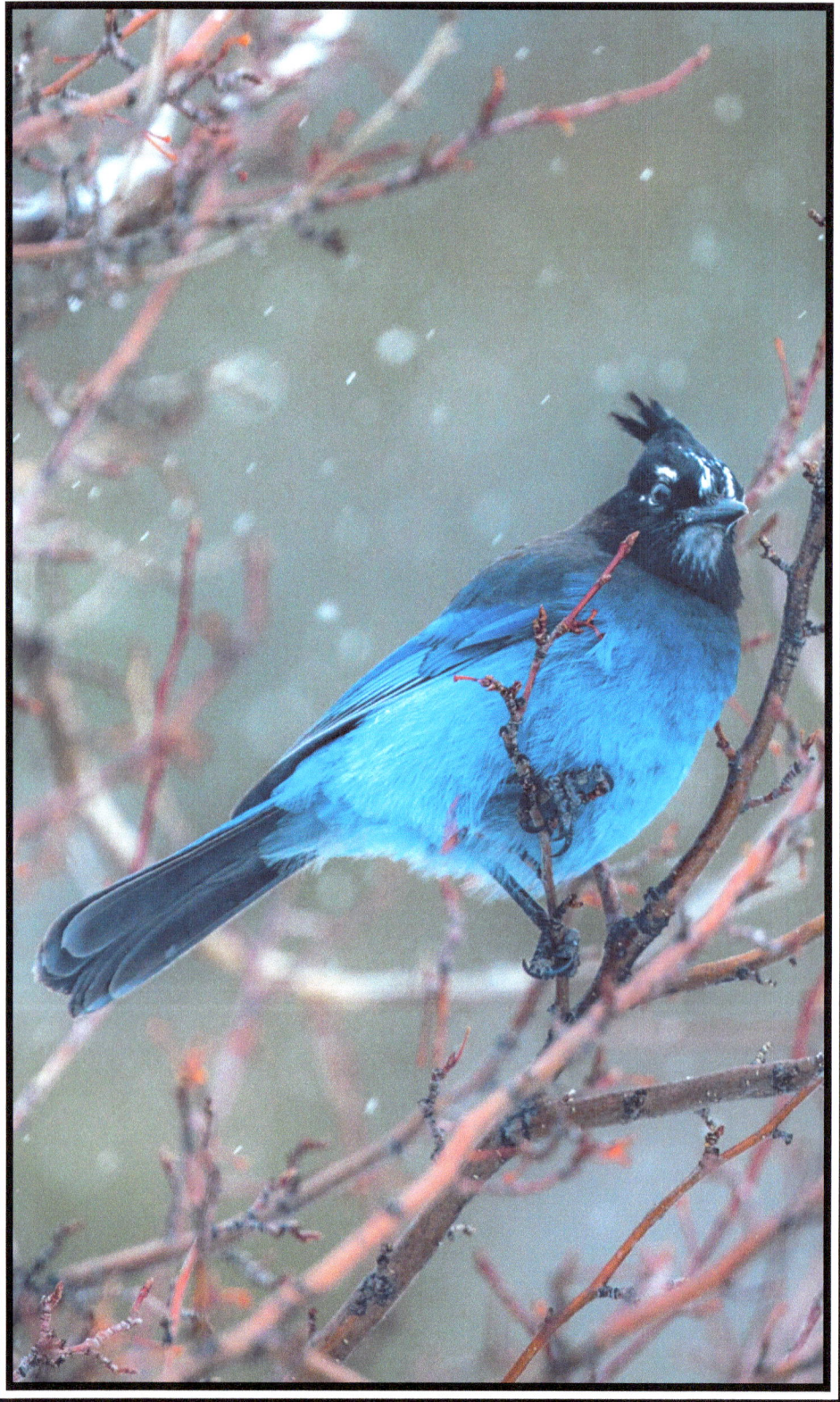

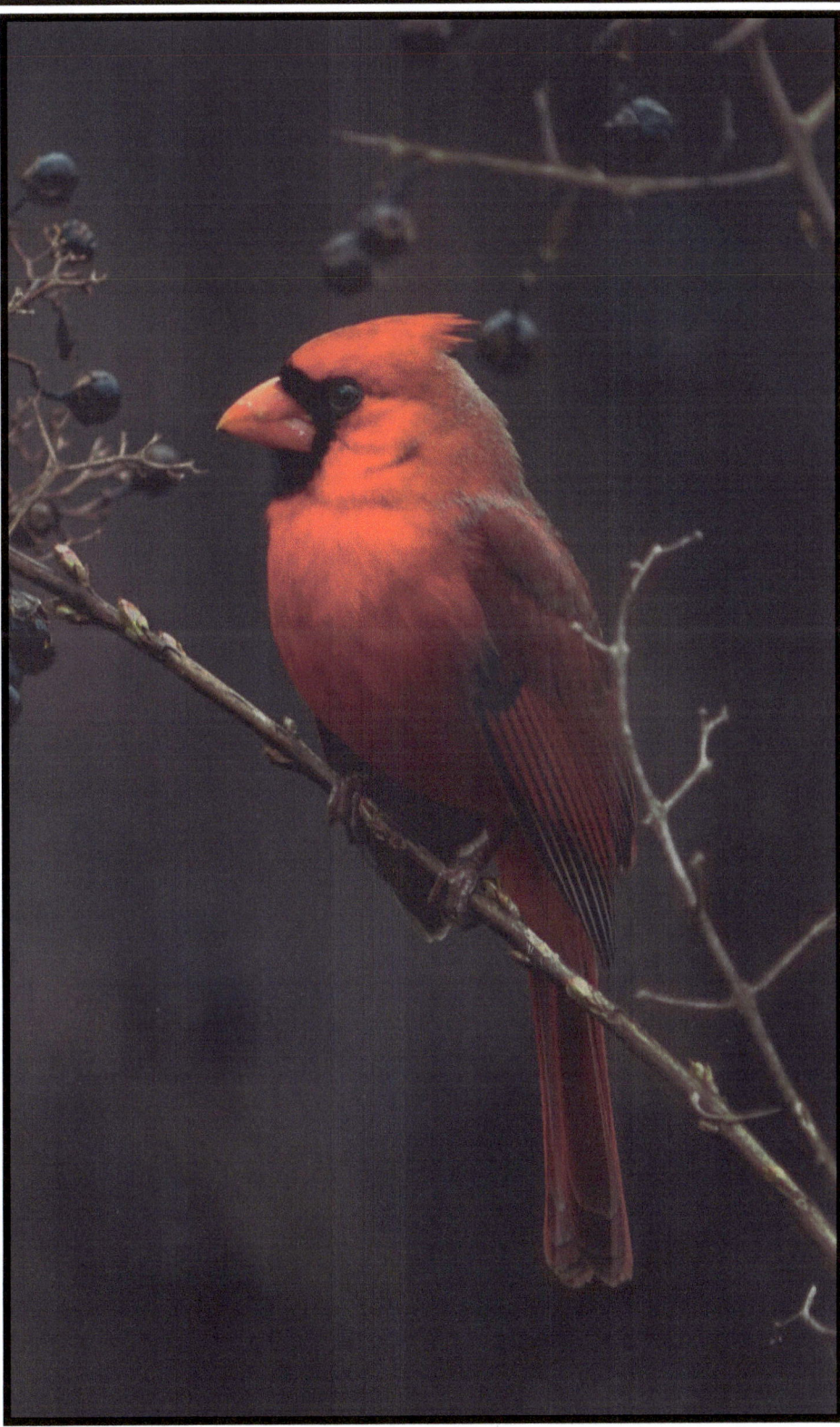

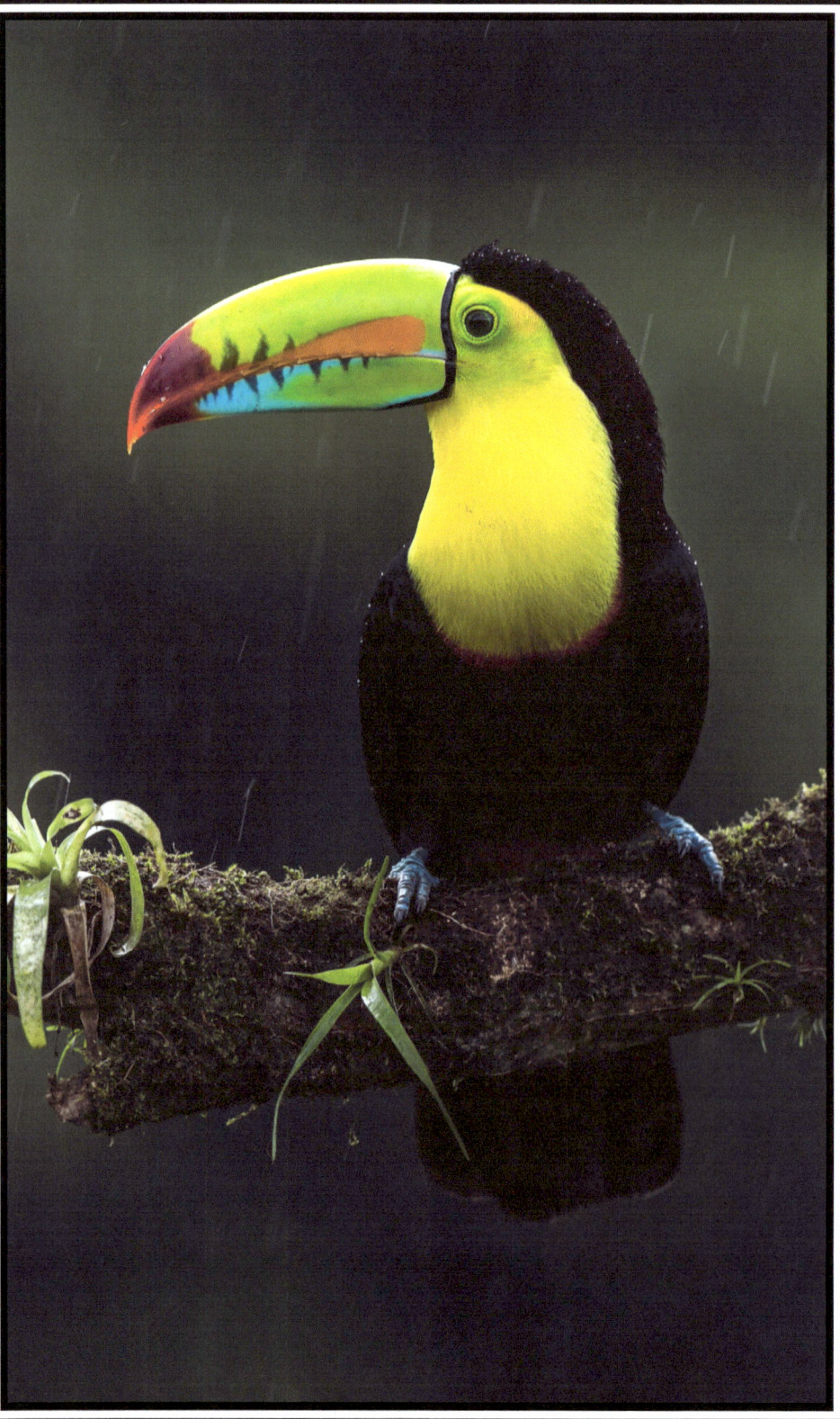

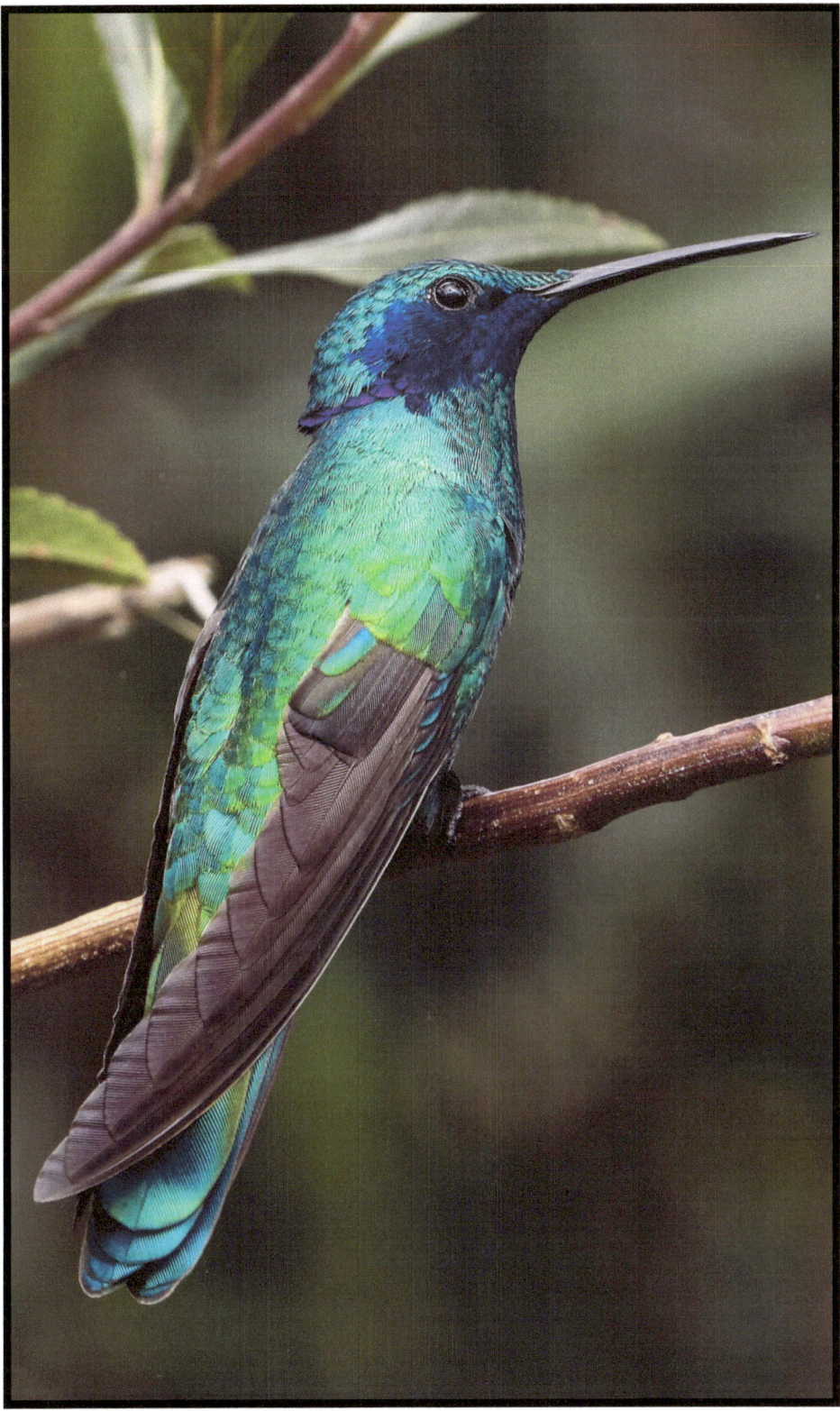

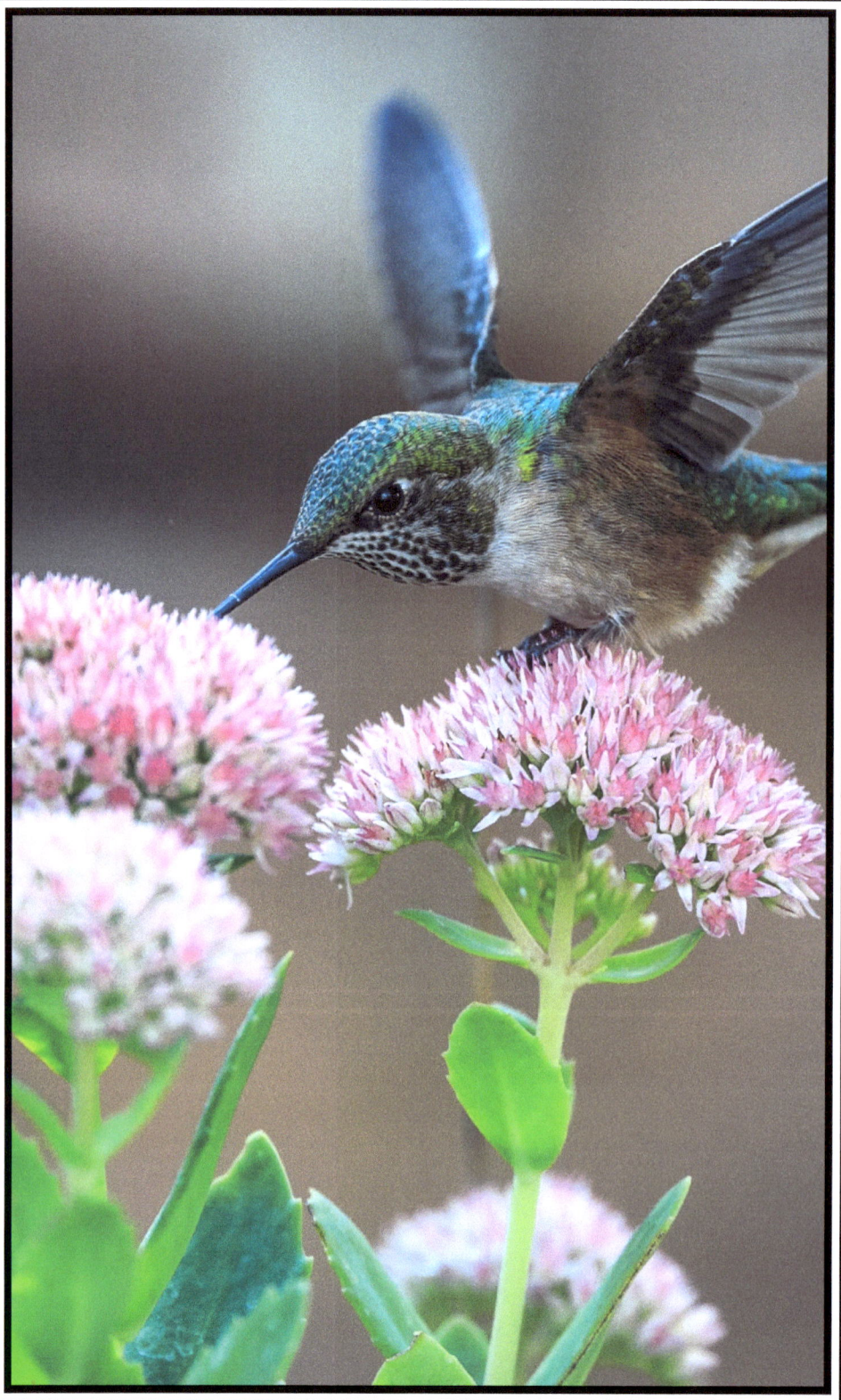

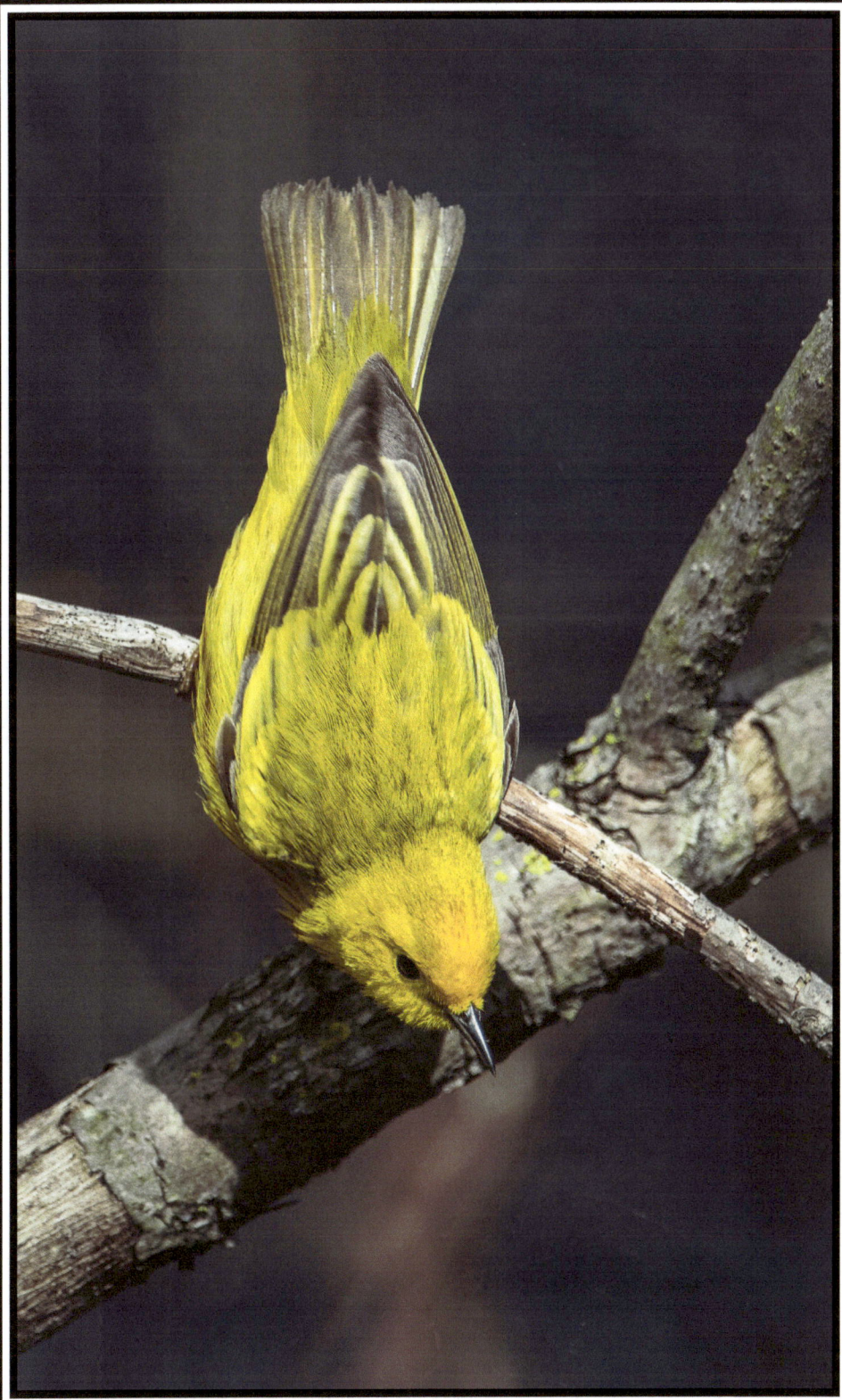

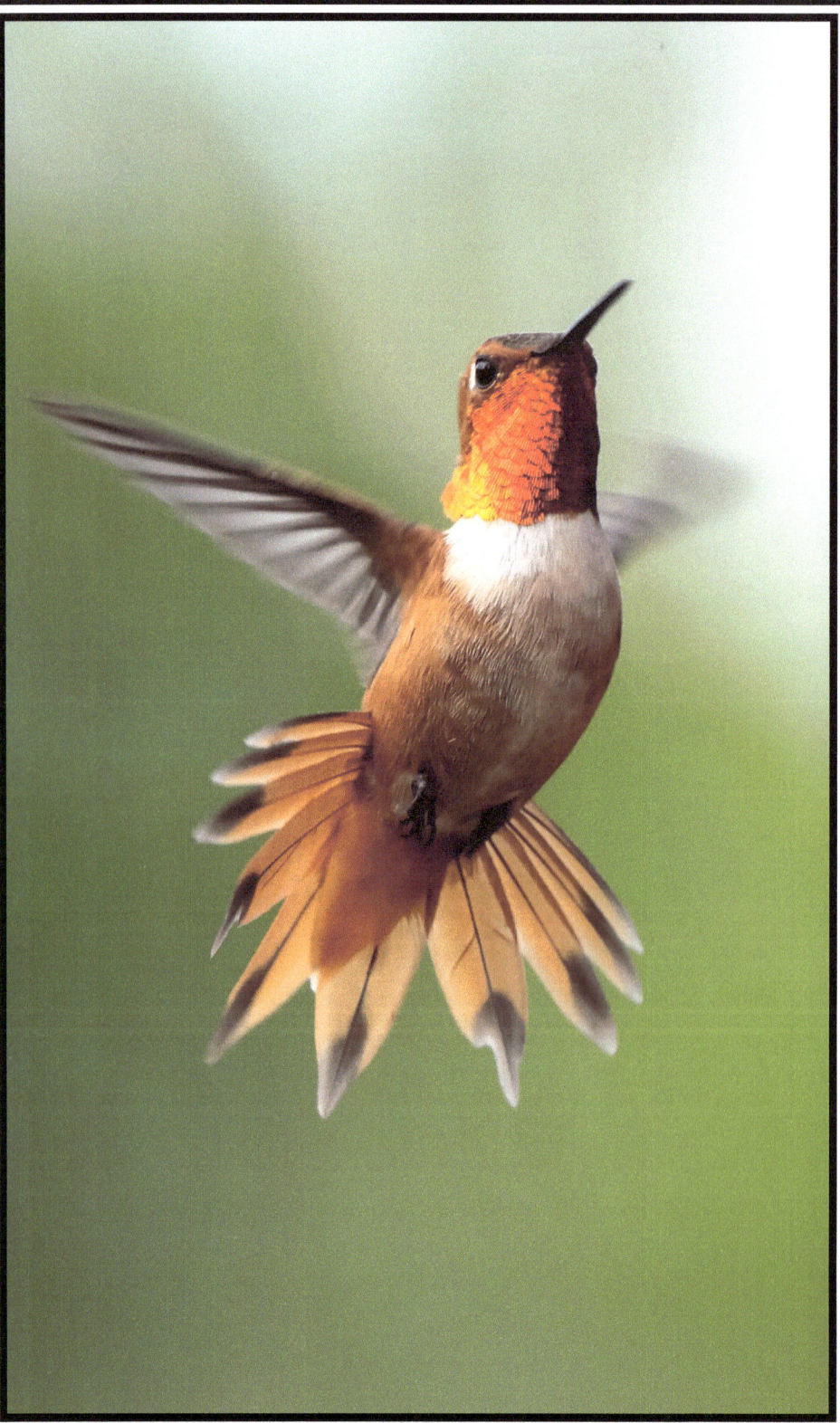

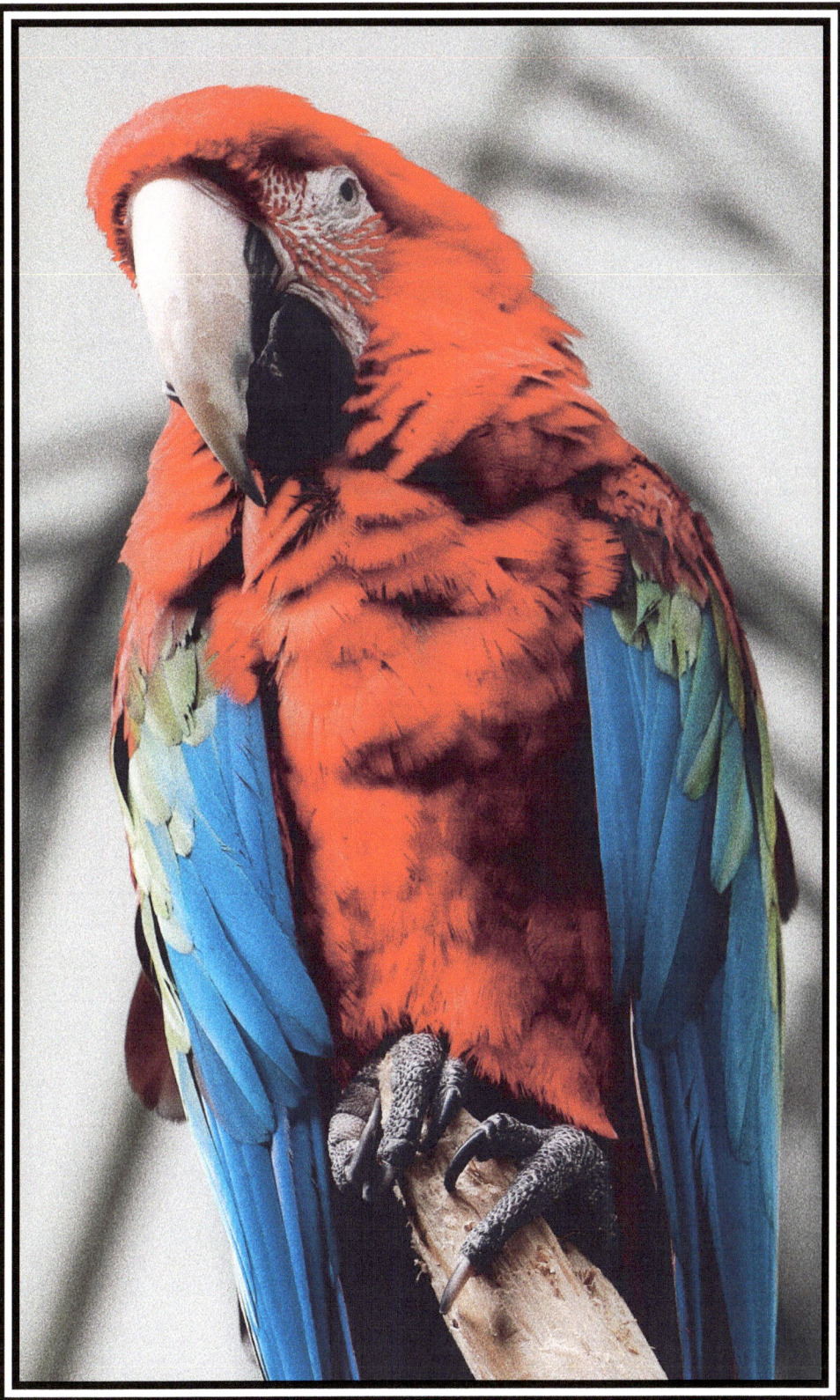

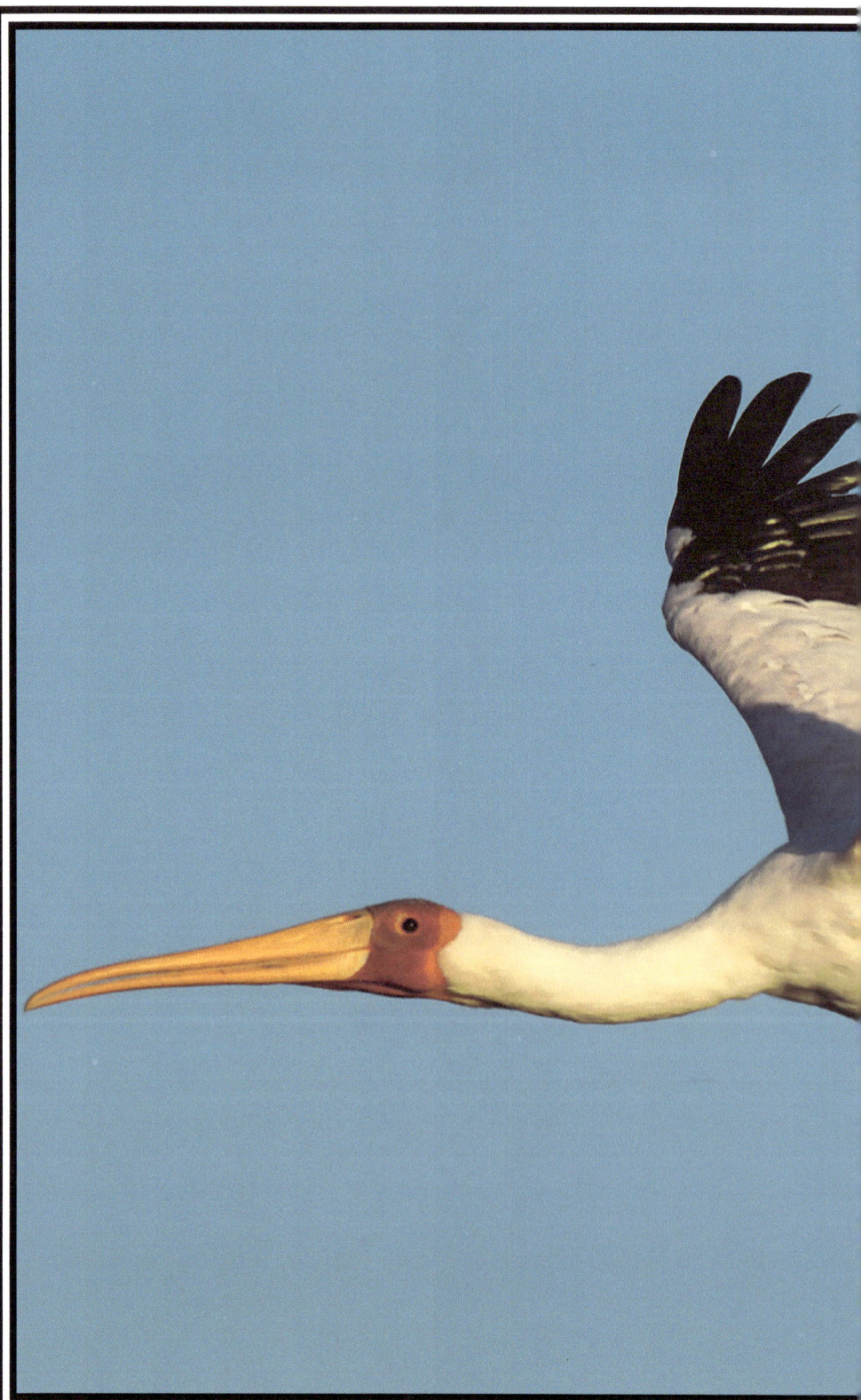

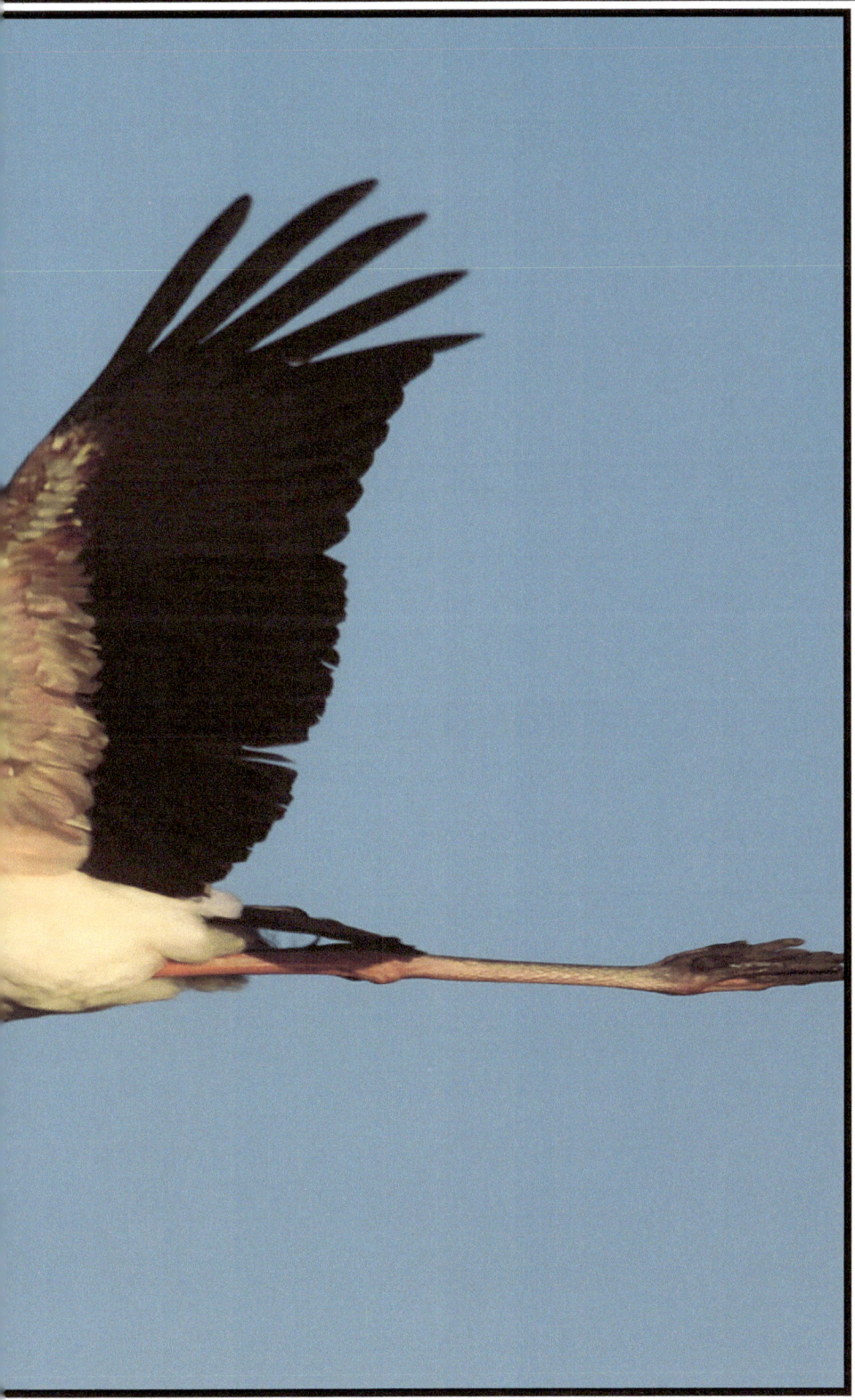

www.ingramcontent.com/pod-product-compliance
Lightning Source LLC
Chambersburg PA
CBHW040336220526
45473CB00009B/2706